CLEVELAND

The Encyclopedia of Cleveland History: Illustrated Volumes
Edited by David D. Van Tassel and John J. Grabowski

1. *Cleveland: A Concise History, 1796–1990,* by Carol Poh Miller and Robert Wheeler

CLEVELAND

A Concise History, 1796–1990

by Carol Poh Miller and Robert Wheeler

INDIANA UNIVERSITY PRESS

Bloomington and Indianapolis

THE PREPARATION OF THIS VOLUME WAS MADE POSSIBLE
BY A GRANT FROM THE CLEVELAND FOUNDATION.

*The paper used in this publication meets the minimum requirements of
American National Standard for Information Sciences—Permanence of
Paper for Printed Library Materials, ANSI Z39.48-1984.*

 ™

Manufactured in the United States of America

Library of Congress Cataloging-in-Publication Data

Miller, Carol Poh
  Cleveland : a concise history, 1796–1990 / by Carol Poh Miller and Robert Wheeler.
    p.   cm.—(The Encyclopedia of Cleveland history ; 1)
  ISBN 0-253-33841-7 (alk. paper). — ISBN 0-253-20572-7 (pbk. : alk. paper)
  1. Cleveland (Ohio)—History.   I. Wheeler, Robert Anthony.
II. Title. III. Series.
F499.C657M55 1990
977.132—dc20

2 3 4 5 94 93 92

                                                                89-24580
                                                                CIP

Contents

Preface   ix

Introduction   1

Part One A COMMERCIAL HAMLET IS FOUNDED

1   Founding and Formation of the Settlement: 1796–1800   7
2   Survival Assured: 1800–1811   15
3   Hamlet as Village: 1812–1824   21

Part Two COMMERCIAL VILLAGE TO COMMERCIAL CITY

4   Canal Village to Provincial Center: 1825–1845   31
5   A National Urban Center Emerges: 1845–1860   49

Part Three RISE OF THE INDUSTRIAL CITY

6   A City Transformed: 1860–1869   69
7   The Industrial Age: 1870–1899   77
8   The Progressive Years: 1900–1914   100
9   Metropolitan Expansion: 1915–1929   113

Part Four TOWARD THE POSTINDUSTRIAL CITY

10   An End to Prosperity: 1930–1939   129
11   War and Renewal: 1940–1949   146

Contents

12 *Exodus and Decline: 1950–1965*   156

13 *The Loss of Confidence: 1966–1979*   166

14 *Comeback City? 1980–1989*   182

   Index   191

ILLUSTRATIONS

Page

8 Moses Cleaveland

11 Plan of Cleveland's Public Square, 1796

12 The Western Reserve, 1798

18 The settlement of Cleaveland, 1800

19 Dunham Tavern, an inn on the road to Buffalo

32 The Ohio & Eric Canal, completed in 1832

35 Cleveland in 1832, looking west from Public Square

37 Map of Cleveland, 1835

40 A triumphal arch on Public Square, Franco-Prussian War

52 Cleveland's Union Depot, completed in 1866

53 Cleveland Rolling Mills blast furnaces, 1880

62 Police precinct station, late nineteenth century

64 James A. Garfield

71 Cleveland's Flats in the 1870s

73 Cleveland's fire department, early twentieth century

74 Cleveland's public transportation system, about 1880

75 Civil War soldiers on Public Square, 1865

80 Millionaires' Row, 1910

81 John D. Rockefeller's summer home in East Cleveland

84 Hiram House float in the 1919 Community Fund parade

90 The Cleveland Rolling Mill Strike of 1885

92 The Visiting Nurse Association assists needy Cleveland families

95 A classroom in Cleveland's public schools, 1917

97 The Arcade: The National Republican League's banquet, 1895

98 Cleveland's Centennial Celebration

104 A backyard in Cleveland's "Big Italy" neighborhood, 1920s

105 Children at the Broadway Branch Library

107 Mayor Tom Johnson inspects street repair, about 1907

111 Cleveland women campaign for the right to vote, 1912

114 Soldiers depart from Union Depot during World War I

115 Watching the Indians win the 1920 World Series

117   Women workers at the Glenn L. Martin plant
119   Ad for housing development for Cleveland's southeast side
119   Plan for housing development for Cleveland's southeast side
122   Newsboys for the *Call and Post*, 1930s
124   The Haymarket district and the Terminal Tower, early 1930s
132   Stone carvers and the Lorain-Carnegie Bridge, 1932
133   A Lorain-Carnegie (Hope Memorial) Bridge pylon, 1932
137   Women protest cutbacks in the WPA program, late 1930s
139   WPA construction project at Brookside Park, 1938
140   Lakeview Terrace public housing project
141   Before Lakeview Terrace
144   The Great Lakes Exposition, 1936, 1937
149   Women at the Cleveland Cadillac Tank Plant, 1944
151   Cleveland's Community Fund supported the U.S.O.
153   Freeways often cut neighborhoods in two
158   The Erieview redevelopment project
161   St. Theodosius Russian Orthodox Cathedral and Valleyview public housing, 1940
168   National Guard troops during the Hough Riots of 1966
170   Carl B. Stokes debates Seth Taft, 1967 mayoral campaign
172   The National Screw & Manufacturing Plant, 1933
173   The National Screw & Manufacturing Plant, 1976
176   George Forbes and Dennis Kucinich, political figures, the 1970s
177   Cleveland hosted the 49th Annual Convention of the NAACP, 1959

While we were editing the *Encyclopedia of Cleveland History*, we made a conscious decision to illustrate the volume only with a limited number of charts and maps. This decision was made in order to preserve space for articles on the many institutions, events, and people who played an important role in the development of the city and who deserved to be included. However, we were conscious that we were missing a form of documentation that has become very important in today's world. Cleveland has an extremely rich store of photographic archives, from the 250,000 images in the library of the Western Reserve Historical Society, to the extensive *Cleveland Press* collection held at the Cleveland State University Library, to the extraordinary Cleveland Picture Collection of the Cleveland Public Library. We hope therefore to offer a series of illustrated volumes drawing on these collections and focused on particular aspects of Cleveland's history, from sports and the fine arts to industry and business, as well as many things in between.

Cleveland: A Concise History, 1796–1990 is the first in this projected series of illustrated histories. It is very appropriate that the first book should be a concise overview of the history of the city of Cleveland. There has been no short history of Cleveland in recent years and none based on the extensive research and the new sources available to authors Carol Poh Miller and Robert Wheeler. They have produced not only an up-to-date and accurate brief history, but also a new synthesis and an interpretation which should enable the reader to understand the political, economic, and cultural growth of the city. It should be a useful guide to teachers of the social studies in the greater Cleveland area secondary schools as well as a tool to enable students to tie important national events and economic and social trends to the local scene, which then may be fleshed out in greater detail by other reading or specific articles from the *Encyclopedia of Cleveland History*.

We have carefully selected the photographs and illustrations to support the authors' text. Wherever possible we have chosen photographs of landmarks that still exist, to orient the reader to the scene at an earlier period of time. We relied on the advice of teachers, but the editors were solely responsible for the final selection.

We wish to thank the many people without whose help this volume could not have been produced. The editors appreciate the work of Beth Johnson and Jimmy Meyer, research assistants who checked much of the information and researched through photographic collections. Sarah Snock, who made contact with the authors and various other people involved in the project, typed and retyped portions of the manuscript. Carol Poh Miller wishes to thank Tom Andrzejewski, Thomas Bier, Gudrun Birnbaum, Robert N. Brown, and Craig S. Miller for valuable advice and suggestions, as well as the staff librarians at the Cleveland Public Library, especially Donald A. Tipka. Robert Wheeler wishes to acknowledge with appreciation the invaluable work of the staff of the library of the Western Reserve Historical Society and especially that of Ann Sindelar.

David D. Van Tassel, *Editor*
Case Western Reserve University

John J. Grabowski, *Editor*
Western Reserve Historical Society

Introduction

I n 1796, shortly after returning to Connecticut from the Western Reserve, Moses Cleaveland, the founder of the city which today bears his name, predicted that, in one person's lifetime, the village would grow to be as large as Old Windham, Connecticut. At the time of that bold prediction, Old Windham had a population of 2,700. And, indeed, after a slow start, Cleveland surpassed that figure by the mid-1830s.

In linking the new settlement to a familiar town in New England, Cleaveland was also making another, unspoken prediction—that the new community would evolve physically, culturally, and economically in a pattern similar to the settlements of New England. Although correct in predicting overall growth, Moses Cleaveland was far off the mark if he indeed felt that his city would grow in the New England mold. While the New England roots of the city's founders have had a profound impact on certain aspects of its history, such as local attitudes toward reform and philanthropy, those roots were already becoming less evident by the time Cleveland surpassed Old Windham in population.

If not a model of New England, Cleveland, as portrayed by the authors of this book, is a composite of the issues and movements that generally constitute American urban history. The story of Cleveland is one of vast economic and social change, as Moses Cleaveland's settlement grew from hamlet to village to city, and finally to a cosmopolitan metropolis bearing little resemblance to Old Windham of New England. Like that of many American cities, Cleveland's history is also a story of abuse and corruption, of reform and charity, and of the unexpected changes a city can undergo when its destiny becomes linked over the years to that of the nation, and eventually to the world and its increasingly interlocked economy. The authors have chosen to divide the history of Cleveland into four major periods, marking the city's movement through these phases of the American experience.

Between 1796 and 1824, Cleveland was a rough frontier settlement eager but initially unsuccessful in its efforts to capitalize on the economic potential its founders perceived in the location on Lake Erie at the mouth of the Cuyahoga River. When, with the construction of the Ohio & Erie Canal, that potential became reality, Cleveland became a typical bustling mercantile center, readily adopting the trappings of civilization as its rough log structures and frontier habits faded into memory. By the end of this second period, 1825–1860, Cleveland was no longer anywhere near the frontier—the American frontier having moved several hundred miles to the west. This merchant city bore little resemblance to a New England town. Its population of over 40,000 was, in large part (44 percent), foreign-born. Its religious life was no longer largely Protestant, but Catholic and Jewish as well. And the close neighborliness of the small town was being rapidly replaced by the anonymity of the large city.

At this time, on the eve of the American Civil War, the city was poised to become a great industrial metropolis. Indeed, its leading citizens had lobbied for more industrial growth during the 1850s so Cleveland would keep up with other American cities on the road to growth and prosperity. Within this next period, 1860–1929, their efforts bore results as Cleveland, with a population of over 800,000 and with an industrial production worth over 1.2 billion dollars, became the nation's fifth-largest city. In accomplishing this, the city covered the remainder of its visible New England heritage with a pall of industrial smoke. By the time of its 125th anniversary, in 1921, a tide of humanity representing over fifty nationalities and races had transformed Cleveland into a city that would have been totally beyond the comprehension of its founder.

During the next sixty years, 1929–1990, Cleveland, like many other American industrial cities, experienced often painful, sometimes violent changes as the nation as a whole moved away from an economy based on heavy industry toward a newer system reliant largely on technology and the provision of services. These changes began with the Depression of the 1930s, and although they were masked by the prosperity of World War II, they again became profoundly evident by the late 1950s. By the 1970s, the city had lost population and, seemingly, faith in its own destiny. Many of its citizens were poor; substantial portions of its once proud neighborhoods stood in disrepair. With such conditions, the city stood in sharp contrast to the many prosperous surrounding suburbs which lured away its citizenry. If Moses Cleaveland could not have correctly envisioned the Cleveland of 1921, few Clevelanders of that later period could have foreseen the changes that would occur in their city within only the next sixty years.

Now, in the late 1980s, as the city moves toward the bicentennial of its founding, it seems to have achieved a renewed sense of pride and a greater faith in its future. Although that future—linked closely to the new international economy—is still not clearly in focus, many of Cleveland's leaders and citizens believe that it will be bright and hopeful and that Cleveland will become one of America's most liveable cities. While Moses Cleaveland, in making his Old Windham statement, predicted a growth in population, Cleveland's leaders of the 1980s look toward a smaller city in the future which will again find its chief economic asset in its location on Lake Erie at the mouth of the Cuyahoga River. The correctness of their predictions can, of course, only be judged by future generations of historians in the same manner in which the authors of this volume have tested those of Moses Cleaveland and other figures in the city's past. We hope, however, that the brief history that follows is not merely a test of past predictions, but a good foundation upon which the reader might stand and look toward the city's future.

Part One

A COMMERCIAL HAMLET IS FOUNDED

Founding and Formation of the Settlement

1796–1800

Explorers of the mouth of the Cuyahoga River and people who reviewed maps of the entire Ohio country lauded the commercial potential of the site of Cleaveland (this spelling was gradually replaced—the modern spelling will be used hereafter). As Moravian missionary John Heckewelder noted in 1796, the area had the best prospect of water communication from Lake Erie to the Ohio River by the Cuyahoga and Muskingum rivers, the only portage being less than 4 miles long. However, despite such promise, a number of early settlers soon had to move away because the miasmic swamps in the floodplain near the river's mouth made them ill. In the words of one pioneer, Jonathan Law, this left a "doleful cloud over the prosperity of Cleveland," which retarded social and economic life until the second decade of the nineteenth century.

Through a series of protracted negotiations, the state of Connecticut had retained rights to western lands granted to it by a seventeenth-century charter. In settlement of this claim, the federal government granted Connecticut the "Western Reserve" tract in the Northwest Territory. Connecticut decided not to administer the land itself and sold it to a hastily gathered group of investors called the Connecticut Land Company in September 1795. The company wasted no time before making arrangements to send a survey party. One of the first jobs of the survey party was to select the site for a capital of the Reserve. First, however, the Indians in the area had to agree that the land was owned by the company, because the grant from the United States did not remove Indian claims. Fortunately for the company, these claims were weakened by a series of battles that took place in western Ohio and ended in the defeat of the Indians at the Battle of Fallen Timbers in the fall of 1794. The treaty that followed reserved for Indian use a rectangular tract beginning at the western bank of the Cuyahoga River and proceeding westward for about 60 miles and south for about 40 miles. The area east and south was open to white settlement. Finally, with only 60 percent of the Reserve available for survey, the Connecticut Land Company sent its surveyors in the spring of 1796.

Moses Cleaveland and the forty-odd members of the party confirmed the company's title to the land in a meeting with the Indians near Buffalo and proceeded to the Reserve, arriving on 4 July. The constitution of the company had directed that the principal town was

This portrait of Moses Cleaveland was painted by artist Rolf Stoll in the 1930s. Like all other portraits of the city's founder, it is based on written descriptions, since no actual likeness of Cleaveland is known to exist. The Western Reserve Historical Society.

to be laid out as quickly as possible. Cleaveland landed at the site of that future town on 22 July but did not then select it; he needed to get "more information of the extent of the ceded land and the traverses of the Lakes and Rivers." He did indicate his early assessment, however: "I believe, as now informed, the Cuyahoga will be the place. It must command the greatest communication either by land or Water of any River on the purchase or in any ceded lands from the head of the Mohawk to the western extent or I am no prophet." Two weeks later, his investigation was complete; he was at the mouth of the river "to lay out [the] capital town," he told Zethan Butterfield on 20 August. When Cleaveland specified *communication* as the chief reason for his decision, he used the word in several ways. His immediate goal was to use the river to transport men, food, and the awkward survey instruments quickly to the interior to continue the survey. Fortunately, it was possible to go up the river 25 miles in a small boat. Had that been his only purpose, he could have established a temporary camp at the mouth of the Cuyahoga, but he laid out the capital there because he saw the commercial prospects of the river, which was navigable for lake sloops for 5 miles and for smaller vessels 10 miles farther if the river was cleared of debris. That was a large "if," because little support for improvements to the river and harbor was forthcoming until the 1820s.

The town was planned to conform to New England and New York models of agricultural villages, because that was the heritage of the surveyors. While the surveyors did their best given their knowledge, other plans that would have incorporated the commercial potential of the area would have been preferable. In any case, the central feature of the plan was a 10-acre public square, which was placed on the plateau near the ridge overlooking the riverbed. The square was divided by Ontario Street, which ran north and south and was 90 feet wide. The east-west street, Superior, was 40 feet wider than Ontario because it led to the riverbank, where most of the river and lake traffic was expected to come into the town. Lots were laid out in an orderly fashion and made ready for sale by 1797, but the "capital" was uninhabited for several years, and only gradually were the plots mapped by Seth Pease and Amos Spafford cleared and settled.

The town format was similar not only to New England villages but also to the main town of the Ohio Land Company, another New England company, which settled a tract in southeastern Ohio along the Ohio River. In 1789, it too laid out a town with wide streets and a formal square, called Marietta. But here the similarity ends. Some of the founders of Marietta had a vision that the town and colony would provide them with an escape from the corruption of the East, and they therefore came to their land as to a refuge. Marietta grew rapidly because of its position near the main avenue of travel for most prospective settlers, the Ohio River. Unlike Cleveland, Marietta had the support of its founders, their presence in the town, and a timely location. Also unlike Cleveland, its prominence faded quickly as lands further along the Ohio successfully attracted settlers.

Consistently throughout its first decade, the Connecticut Land Company demonstrated that its primary goal was not settlement but quick sale for profit. Little encouragement was given to settlers, and no improvements were granted by the company to the capital site. In fact, other than a crude road cut through the woods from the Pennsylvania border to Cleveland, the company was interested only in land distribution. To that end, as soon as the final surveys were completed, tracts were chosen by lottery in January 1798. At the same time, the company gave lots in Cleveland to several early residents because their presence encouraged other, paying settlers. The lottery system itself made settlement haphazard, since investors picked land of varying qualities from separate boxes, which prevented them from owning contiguous tracts. Therefore, settlement of the entire Reserve was not orderly, and Cleveland, on the western edge of open land, was even more isolated.

The model used in much of the original settlement of New England and of Marietta required that towns be inhabited first, so that a community was created. The plan used in the Western Reserve, however, was designed for quick sale without regard for the creation of communities. Consequently it took longer to settle the towns on the Reserve, especially those not on its eastern edge near travel routes. Some adventurous settlers did come to the area before 1800. They were rugged frontier types, more interested in trade with Indians and in providing

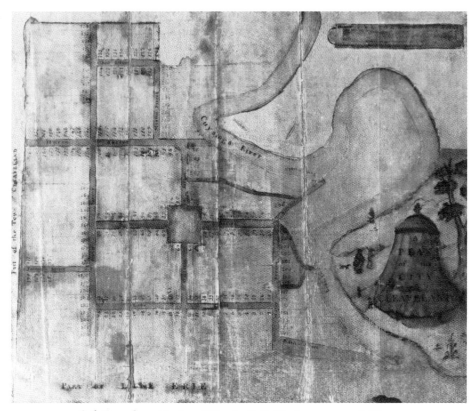

Seth Pease drew this plan of Cleveland's Public Square in 1796. The plan shows the Square from the north (looking south). The Western Reserve Historical Society.

Seth Pease's map of 1798 shows the extent of the initial survey of the Western Reserve. The lands west of the Cuyahoga River were still subject to Indian claims and had not been surveyed. The Western Reserve Historical Society.

supplies for newcomers than they were in becoming farmers. The typical inhabitants during these first years did not stay long near the river: they either left the area altogether or moved to nearby townships, away from the sickness that had begun to affect those who stayed near the village site. The most notable resident of these early years was Lorenzo Carter, who built a large log cabin where others could lodge and who quickly controlled most of the Indian trade. Others, such as James Kingsbury, Nathaniel Doan, and Ezekiel Hawley, came and liked the general area but moved out of the immediate Cleveland area. In April 1800, Lorenzo Carter was the only resident of Cleveland.

CHAPTER TWO

Survival Assured

1800–1811

While the number of immigrants to the Reserve did not meet the expectations of the Connecticut Land Company, towns such as Warren had begun to grow significantly. In all of the Reserve, according to the federal census of 1800, there were 1,500 people. Ten years later, the number had grown to 17,000 in the Reserve, but to only ten families in Cleveland. The reasons for this discrepancy are found in the pattern of migration from the East and in the problems with the site. Land in the Western Reserve was owned by residents of Connecticut, but most of them were content to remain landholders rather than become colonists in the new territory. Therefore, northeastern Ohio was not settled wholly by or even by a majority of settlers from Connecticut. Many residents were from other New England states, and 20 percent were from New York. Apparently, those in upper New England (Vermont and New Hampshire) as well as those from western Massachusetts were more likely to move in the early years of the century. These areas had been opened for settlement after the Revolutionary War, and many who went there did not find the prosperity they had hoped to achieve. Therefore, they were willing to move. Sometimes they moved to New York State first, and then on to the Reserve.

Fortunately, there were positive signs that Cleveland would be a political center, which helped bolster long-term prospects. First, the entire Western Reserve was declared part of the United States in 1800, which opened the way for formal political organization. The same year, Trumbull County was created to encompass the Reserve, with Warren as its county seat. Significantly, Cleveland was made one of the eight townships in the county. Although it would have been proper to name Cleveland the county seat, there was little population at the site, and, therefore, little need for a county seat in the area. It was also likely that new counties would be created quickly. Trumbull County formed part of the new state of Ohio, admitted to the union in 1803. Just two years later, Geauga County was formed from a portion of Trumbull. In 1807, the state legislature created Cuyahoga County, and, after some debate, Cleveland was named the county seat in 1809 over the objections of its more populous neighbor, Newburgh. One additional form of recognition came when the federal government made Cleveland a port of entry in 1805 and appointed a collector to monitor trade from Canada as well as lake and river traffic. These political changes added formal government responsibilities and officers to implement them. Throughout this early period, the primary political divisions were the township and the county: no formal offices were created for the hamlet itself. The earliest governmental positions ensured that local elections were properly run and that the basic rules of government were observed. Because there were relatively few adult males in the entire township, many of them served in several offices simultaneously. Most eligible voters participated in early elections even though the process of voting seems to have been carefully and rigorously monitored. Jonathan Law noted in his diary on 11 October 1802 that he had attended an election in Warren where "every man was particularly questioned with respect to his qualifications as a voter. Many were examined & many offended. Every man's vote was examined by the judges & then put into the box." Similar care was probably taken at Cleveland, where as many as three judges and two clerks presided at each election.

Several factors combined to inhibit long-term settlement in Cleveland. Early on, a conflict emerged between the rough group of settlers who lived "under the hill" near the river and those who thought the group was detrimental to the development of Cleveland. Samuel Huntington wrote to Moses Cleaveland on 10 February 1802 that it was difficult to convince prospective settlers to stay, because Lorenzo Carter informed them that the harbor would never be opened and "that nothing can be made by trade . . . at the same time he is clearing $1000 per annum by his Indian Trade." Moreover, Carter "gathers about him all the itinerant Vagabonds that he meets with, out of whom he gets all his labour done for their board and Whiskey: over whom he has an absolute control—organizing a phalanx of Desperadoes and setting all Laws at defiance." Gideon Granger included these fears in a letter he wrote on 20 October 1804 declaring his intention to settle in the Reserve. He said, "Cleveland has a Thousand Charms but I am deterred from pitching on that place by the Sickness, the poorness of the Soil and the Inhabitants under the hill." Granger correctly identified the most important factor limiting the size of the hamlet—sickness. The most prevalent disease, described by contemporaries as fever and ague, was malaria, which affects its victims over a long period of time and debilitates them so they are more susceptible to other diseases. The Cuyahoga had changed its course to a new channel before the beginning of white settlement, and the abandoned channel had formed an extensive pool of stagnant water, which bred the mosquitoes that carried the disease. Some residents observed that dry seasons reduced the problem, but none knew the cause or the cure.

In the wake of these realities, the population of the area grew slowly, which retarded institutional development and stunted economic progress. From 1802 to 1810, the township grew from 76 adult males (or about 200 people) to 300 people, and the hamlet itself managed only 57 residents by 1810. Political institutions were established quickly, but social and economic structures lagged behind. There were some cultural stirrings in 1811 when a local lending library was formed by sixteen of the eighteen families in Cleveland, and when the Freemasons established a group. Formal schools would not appear until later, and no churches were organized, so the settlers relied on the occasional visits of missionary clergy such as Joseph Badger. Residents were hampered in their attempts to prosper economically, be-

This sketch by Captain Allen Gaylord shows the struggling settlement of Cleaveland on the east bank of the Cuyahoga River in 1800. It is the earliest known view of the settlement. The Western Reserve Historical Society.

cause most were still in debt for their land and had not recovered from the expense involved in moving. In addition, they were forced to pay exorbitant prices for what they needed, although they had no way to earn money. The company turned a deaf ear to requests such as the one made by Samuel Huntington on 15 November 1801 for funds to improve the harbor so that "our Salt, Iron, Potash, and Sugar Kettles and such Bulky articles" would cost less to buy and so that "we might supply the Ohio Country, if we had a harbour for Vessels, cheaper than they can be supplied from Pitt." Without this help from the company, most residents planted crops in the marginal soil and bartered locally, for there was little hard money on the Reserve. They were aided by several local mills that ground flour and produced rough boards. Apart from these mills, the first signs of commercial life were

Dunham Tavern, an early inn on the road (Euclid Avenue) to Buffalo, was already considered a "relic" of Cleveland's past when this picture was taken in the 1920s. The Western Reserve Historical Society.

the establishment of a merchant store in 1808 and the building of several lake vessels. One other positive sign was the opening of several communication links with other areas. In 1806, the company funded a road that connected Buffalo with the eastern boundary of its lands at the Pennsylvania border, where that road joined the road to Cleveland. Impetus was provided for other roads when the western portion of the Reserve, which remained in Indian hands, opened for settlement as the result of a treaty in 1805. A road through this section, from Cleveland to the Huron River, opened four years later. In addition, Elijah Gun operated a ferry across the Cuyahoga to aid travelers and settlers. For all these reasons, the potential of the capital had grown, for it was now in the center of the Western Reserve.

On the eve of the War of 1812, Jonathan Law's "doleful cloud" still hung over Cleveland. When John Melish described the hamlet in 1811, he noted that Cleveland had only a few houses—"16 dwellings, 2 taverns, 2 stores, 1 school." Its trade "was limited to salt, a little flour, pork, whiskey," and the river, clogged with sand, was "stagnant, foul, & putrid smelling."

CHAPTER THREE

Hamlet as Village

1812–1824

During the twelve years that ended in 1824, Cleveland became a community with an adequate social and institutional base, a supportive political structure, and an economy poised to expand rapidly. Jessie Harris wrote home to Vermont in 1824 that Cleveland was a thriving town with nine stores and three taverns. He added that there were six vessels owned in Cleveland constantly sailing the lakes and that all kinds of merchandise could be bought. He concluded by noting that a canal from the Ohio River was scheduled to enter Lake Erie at the village site. Increased lake traffic and the likelihood of a canal terminus meant a total of 500 residents by 1825.

The population of all of Cleveland Township was only 605 in 1820. Much has been made of this small population in comparison to the populations of other townships in the Western Reserve. Cleveland was easily outnumbered by the townships of Ashtabula, Painesville, Warren, and by several other townships, including Chagrin Falls, Newburgh, and Euclid, within Cuyahoga County. However, Cleveland was about twice the size of the average township in the Reserve and its population increase of 260 percent was typical of the entire region over the previous ten years. The characteristics of its people indicated its current and future role. The entire Reserve, Cleveland in particular, had a young population, but Cleveland Township had more adults under 46 and fewer children than the region in general. This workforce was unique in the county, being only about one-third agricultural while the county average was over four-fifths agricultural. The majority of county residents involved in commercial and manufacturing activities lived in Cleveland. All village officers in 1820 listed commerce or industry as the major work of their households, not farming. Though not the most populous township in Cuyahoga County or in the Reserve, Cleveland was the most significant commercial and manufacturing force in the area.

Several social and cultural institutions were founded in the years after the close of the War of 1812, and political recognition of the hamlet as a village was successfully promoted in 1815. The four churches founded between 1815 and 1820 helped to dispel Cleveland's reputation as irreligious. That same year, a Sunday school opened to keep idle boys off the streets on the Sabbath, and within its first three months, thirty "scholars" attended weekly classes in reading, appearance, and behavior. Traditional schools were also founded during this time but were funded privately, since taxpayers were unwilling to take on the additional financial burden. A more socially motivated school designed for adults promised dancing lessons to students in 1820. Other cultural opportunities ranged from traveling exhibitions to a series of lectures on topics of the day. Play readings and amateur dramatic presentations took place, including weekly performances by a group called the Wags of Cleveland at the Shakespeare Gallery. Displays of wax figures and a demonstration of gas were licensed by the village in the 1820s. By far the most impressive secular cultural institution was the Cleveland Forum, which held weekly meetings during the winter. Subjects for 1823 included "Is Love a Stronger Passion than Hatred?" "Are Agricultural Societies Beneficial?" "Ought the United States to Tax Unmarried Men over Thirty?" and "Is Slander Cause of More Mischief than Flattery?" One of the topics clearly met with approval, since, in May 1823, the first meeting of the agricultural society was called. It was timed to coincide with the Court of Common Pleas session in Cleveland, which would bring a large number of people to the village. Many informal social contacts were made at these sessions, where much business of all kinds took place. In sum, by 1824 these activities reflected a significant change from the frontier survival period. Furthermore, Cleveland had a newspaper, begun in 1818, which informed the growing local community and acted as an advocate of Cleveland's growing importance.

As cultural activities increased, the social structure of the area became more differentiated. One observer noted that most Clevelanders did not dress fashionably. He found the typical dress of Cleveland women rather plain, and that men generally dressed in homespun cloth except on special days. However, some men and women did dress with good taste, many of whom were political and commercial leaders of the town. At the other end of Cleveland's social spectrum, which admittedly was not as broad as that in eastern society, a number of poor appeared. The township warned several families to leave its jurisdiction to prevent their becoming dependent on the village and it later paid for the removal of one family and for the funeral of another person. In addition to court days, the Fourth of July brought many members of the fledgling community together, perhaps because it celebrated both the founding of the nation and the date when Moses Cleaveland and his party entered the Reserve in 1796. Such events were elaborate celebrations for the time. Village leaders met to plan a Fourth of July celebration in 1819 in which all residents were invited to join the procession from Merwin's Hotel to the courthouse to hear the Declaration of Independence recited by Reuben Wood, Esq., and then to enjoy dinner at the Commercial Coffee House. Two years later, a list of Fourth of July celebrations in the *Herald* included three separate events for the area. Clearly, these events differed in tone from the early social problems between those who lived "under the hill" and other residents.

Cultural opportunities and social differentiation complemented political changes, which gave the hamlet a measure of autonomy when it became a village in 1815. This new status required a village administrative structure, including a president, three trustees, a recorder, a treasurer, and a marshal. While the title of village was new, prominent politicians already knew who would be appropriate officeholders in the new structure, and consequently the offices went to a small number of people. With the exception of the first year, there was only one treasurer before 1825, Ashbel Walworth. Two men, Daniel Kelley and Leonard Case, served all but two of the ten years as president of the village; Horace Perry was recorder for the 1810s, and Eleazar Waterman from 1821 to 1825. Horace Perry was recorder from 1815 to 1819, president in 1820, and a trustee from 1821 to 1825. During these same years, he also served the township as treasurer for three years, as justice of the peace for seven years, as clerk for three years, and finally as trustee for two years. Clearly, Perry was one of the most important decision makers in Cleveland before 1825. Taken as a group, village officeholders were important economic leaders in both commerce and manufacturing.

Perry and his peers passed a series of rules governing the hamlet, which guaranteed a more orderly society and signaled the gradual end of the frontier period. In the village's early years, residents recorded earmarks that identified their animals, but by 1820 animals were a nuisance in the village, and a set of ordinances regulated them. For instance, swine and cattle could not run in the streets, stray geese could be killed, and horse races were banned. Social controls prohibited discharging firearms or obstructing village officers. Economic regulations required all weights and measures to be sealed by the village inspector and all residents to use the hay scales, also run by the village inspector. The village fathers ruled that parents were liable for offenses their children committed. While these measures did not ensure a peaceful, obedient society, they did suggest that most villagers preferred order to the disorder of the early years.

Village politics during this period were service-oriented, with few real rivalries. The most active races and the most significant political activity occurred on county, state, and national levels. Cleveland was the site of many political meetings to form slates of candidates for upcoming elections. Each township in the county sent two delegates to a county convention in 1818 to select a slate of candidates, for instance. Later the group published their preferred list in the Cleveland paper. On the national level, John Sloane ran against Peter Hitchcock for Congress from the area. Although Sloane lacked local support and received few local votes, he won the election.

State political activities were most important to the future of the hamlet, since both political advances and major works projects were controlled by the legislature. For instance, the efforts of Alfred Kelley, a state legislator from Cleveland, resulted in the hamlet's designation as a village with an autonomous political structure in 1815. Residents began to request aid through their representatives for harbor improvements and for links with southern Ohio as early as the beginning of the nineteenth century. Proposals for funds to open a road to the south and to build a canal over the portage between the Tuscarawas and the Cuyahoga were presented, as were various plans to open the harbor. Generally, these requests failed. However, the most economically important one, the location of the canal terminus, succeeded after years of impatience. The idea was an old one, but the state legislature first seriously considered a canal proposal in 1817, the same year construction began on the Erie Canal in New York. Two years later, legislation to incorporate a company to build a canal between Lake Erie and the Ohio River was before the state senate. After weeks of speculation on the great benefits this canal would bring to Cleveland, the *Herald* reported in February 1819 that the bill was lost because the legislature had appointed several engineers to identify all practical routes. Fortunately for the Cleveland area, Alfred Kelley, a state legislator from Cleveland, served on the new commission. Over the next several years, each potential route from the lake to the river was surveyed. The politics were so intense that Kelley asked the *Herald* in 1822 not to publish news on the canal commission because it created regional jealousies, and he assured the public that no decision had been made. It would not be until February 1825 that the final decision to locate the northern terminus where the Cuyahoga empties into Lake Erie was announced. While lake traffic would have continued to come to Cleveland, the location of the northern gateway in Cleveland was crucial to the quick rise in its fortunes. The positive impact that discussion of the canal had on the village and its economic prospects was enormous and was undoubtedly the product as much of political influence as of sound engineering judgment.

Political help from the national level came slowly. As early as 1818, the village petitioned Congress for funds to improve the harbor but failed. Consequently, all passengers and goods were landed on the shore in light boats. Six years later, Congress did allocate money for a lighthouse on Lake Erie, but at Grand River, not at Cleveland. Efforts to obtain funds to remove the sandbars and to build a public pier would wait until after 1824. Despite these setbacks, the economic history of Cleveland from 1812 to 1824 improved significantly after a shaky start. The War of 1812 helped Cleveland become a trade center, since supplies were stored in the hamlet and soldiers camped near the town, but the Panic of 1818 hurt economic opportunity, because it made barter pervasive and credit difficult to obtain. Finally, in the 1820s the "doleful cloud" over economic affairs lifted noticeably as lake traffic increased and the canal discussion intensified. Evidence of prosperity was nearly everywhere by the mid-1820s. The port of Cleveland was thriving by 1824, when exports exceeded $38,000 and imports $196,000; in 1809, total exports were only $50.

Cleveland became the commercial center of Cuyahoga County during these years. The expansion took two paths: wholesale and retail trade and lake traffic. Trading posts were replaced by stores in growing numbers after the War of 1812, and merchants built warehouses as early as 1815. The next year the Commercial Bank of Lake Erie opened, partially to finance business and commercial operations. While no specific proof is available, there is little doubt that this bank gave Cleveland an advantage over its rivals, since it became the focal point of important economic decisions. Predictably, the bank failed in the aftermath of the national Panic of 1818. The shortage of hard currency was acute in the late 1810s, and the village issued corporation shinplasters or script (privately issued paper currency), to help residents pay taxes. Twenty businessmen, a considerable number given the small size of the hamlet, signed a notice informing the public that they would not accept the script. Retail outlets expanded during the early 1820s as furniture, books, shoes, and general merchandise of all sorts sold in the village. No doubt sales increased, because the first bridge linking the east and west banks of the Cuyahoga opened in 1822. By 1824 there were many local merchants selling eastern goods to local residents.

Significantly, the lake trade was also increasing in the late 1810s.

At the peak of the shipping season in mid-July 1818, twenty-one boats entered or cleared the port for Buffalo and Detroit. Indicative of the lack of significant exports, they transported household goods, stoneware, dry goods, whiskey, livestock, pork, flour, butter, grindstones, and tallow. A ropewalk opened to supply rigging and other necessities to expanding shipping and boatbuilding enterprises. A new era in water travel arrived in Cleveland in 1818 as the first steamboat, *Walk-in-the-Water*, arrived and was visited by a number of gentlemen and ladies from the village. The village entered the steamboat era with the launching of the 250-ton *Enterprise* in 1824. By the end of this initial stage of development, Cleveland was economically tied more to the lake than to the river, since most of its gross imports and exports came from the lake. Fortunately, it had all the necessary mercantile and financial institutions in place ready to meet any increased demand.

Physical changes in the village mirrored its hopeful, if ambivalent, economic position. In 1814, Cleveland had a total of thirty-four dwellings and business places. After 1815, development first occurred between Public Square and the river, then proceeded south of Superior and east across Ontario. By 1824, separate residential districts began to emerge, with mansions built north of Superior toward the lake, west of Ontario, and around Public Square. All of these changes removed neither Cleveland's rustic appearance nor its "doleful cloud," but the groundwork was complete for the emergence of a commercial city.

RW

Part Two

COMMERCIAL VILLAGE TO COMMERCIAL CITY

CHAPTER FOUR

Canal Village to Provincial Center
1825–1845

The first twenty years of Cleveland's emergence as a city began with the construction of the canal and ended with the return of good times after a protracted depression, which began in 1837. In the process, a town developed that controlled its hinterland economically and was the focal point for culture and politics in northeastern Ohio. Change happened rapidly during the era: in 1825 "the west" was near Cleveland, in 1845 it was a thousand miles away; in 1825 Cleveland had a predominately native population, in 1845 half the city's residents were foreign-born; in 1825 political officeholders served out of self-perceived duty, in 1845 party politics controlled many elections; in 1825 most of those in the village knew each other, in 1845 anonymity replaced familiarity. By far the most important single factor in the era was the transformation of the economy, for it drove all the other changes. Four events in 1825 determined the economic future of the village. First, in large part through the efforts of Alfred Kelley, the state of Ohio agreed to locate the northern terminus of the Ohio & Erie Canal at the mouth of the Cuyahoga River. Almost immediately, eastern funds began pouring into the village to take advantage of the predicted boom. Second, Clevelanders watched the progress of the Erie Canal closely and celebrated its completion in October with a dinner. More important, the *Herald* reported on 25 November that a "procession of about 20 carts laden with the produce of the western country, brought from Lake Erie through the canal passed through several streets of New York city . . . carrying appropriate flags and banners. The produce was from Detroit, from Sandusky, from Cleveland, from Buffalo. . . ." For the near future, Cleveland did not need the Ohio Canal, because the village served as a gathering place where local farmers sent their produce destined for Buffalo, and ultimately for New York City. Moreover, the completion of the Erie Canal freed contractors and workers experienced in canal construction to come to Cleveland and begin work.

A third event that contributed to Cleveland's economic future was its selection as the site of the northern terminus of the canal. Engineers determined late in 1825 that a west-side route would be less expensive if a wooden aqueduct were built to take the canal across the river 4 miles south of Cleveland. Public opinion, stated the *Herald* on

Begun in 1825 and completed in 1832, the Ohio & Erie Canal linked Cleveland with Portsmouth on the Ohio River. This picture was taken nearly eighty years after the canal was completed. The Western Reserve Historical Society.

19 November, "cannot be mistaken, it is decidedly and unquestionably in favor of the eastern route." The final decision in favor of the east bank was made by the end of the year and sealed the relationship between the two sides of the river, retarding west-side development and ensuring the supremacy of the village of Cleveland. Fourth, efforts to obtain money from the federal government for harbor improvements finally succeeded when $5,000 was appropriated, undoubtedly to accommodate the increased shipping requirements of the canal. With another, larger grant two years later, engineers successfully opened a new straight channel to the lake. The swift-flowing river eliminated the sandbars that had blocked the harbor for lakegoing vessels and removed the miasmic swamps from the mouth, which lifted the "doleful cloud" of sickness from the village.

The prosperity canal promoters had hoped for was confirmed by developments over the next twenty years. With improved transportation and reduced freight rates, demand for agricultural products increased along with farm productivity and prices, which, in turn, enticed more people to move to the hinterland and gave areas close to the canal a marked advantage over their rivals. In the process, the canal replaced the river route to New Orleans as a major conduit for goods headed to the East Coast from the Old Northwest Territory. Cleveland benefited particularly because it was the terminal point and a growing lake port. It collected produce as it came north and sent manufactured goods south. Often overlooked is that Cleveland's hinterland did not include much of the Western Reserve, because it followed the canal route south to Akron, Columbus, and the Ohio River and passed through only two Reserve counties, Cuyahoga and Summit. The Cleveland-Akron portion of the canal was the first scheduled for completion, and construction contracts were issued quickly. As workers poured in, the cash they received for wages replaced the local barter economy and increased the number of bank notes in circulation, thereby facilitating economic transactions. Within the year, hogs driven to Cleveland were slaughtered and sent east, and the latest goods from New York appeared in local stores. Cleveland had become "a mart of business for this section of the country," according to the charter of Western Reserve College in 1826. Forwarding and commission agents arrived to send property anywhere, sell it in any market, and advance funds for property deposited with them. On 4 July 1827, less than two years after construction had begun, the first canal boat arrived in Cleveland from Akron with the governor and other distinguished citizens on board and was greeted by a large number of spectators who lined the hills and banks. Five years later the canal was finally completed; Cleveland traded with the region from Columbus north, while goods south of the state capital went to the Ohio River.

From 1827 to 1840, the Ohio Canal was the exclusive avenue to the lake and to canal connections to the east. The first year, flour, ashes, and butter and cheese came north, while salt, lumber, and over half a million pounds of merchandise went south from the village. As the canal pushed inland, the amount of merchandise grew to over three million pounds in 1830, to ten million in 1834, and to a high of nineteen million by 1838. As wheat prices jumped from approximately thirty cents per bushel before the canal to over sixty cents in 1833, the amount of flour and wheat transshipped at Cleveland jumped eight times by 1840, when over two million bushels of wheat and half a million barrels of flour arrived via the canal. Significantly, the town's grain trade was almost totally dependent on this traffic; for example, in 1841, of the 461,000 barrels of flour shipped from Cleveland, 441,000 arrived by canal. By 1840, 44 percent of Ohio's wheat and flour came from the "wheat belt," a group of counties north and east of Columbus, making Cleveland the focus of the principal grain market of the Great Lakes. The other major agricultural products, corn and pork, rose at slightly less impressive levels.

Newspapers followed the rapid rise in local fortunes. The *Herald* commented in May 1830 that the amount of goods received by canal had already surpassed that of 1829 because of the abundant harvest and confidence in the canal. Seven years later, the *Cleveland Herald and Gazette* observed that in 1832 much of the local economy had been limited to barter, and few farm products other than beeswax, pot and pearl ashes, and feathers were exported, whereas now "the rich products of the interior [are] floating along" the docks. Enticed by canal products and aided by harbor improvements, more and more lake vessels arrived and cleared. From a beginning of 350 arrivals and departures in 1831, the annual number rose to 1,000 by the late 1830s, and to nearly 1,600 by 1844, exclusive of steamboats. Vessels increased in both number and size throughout the period. Nearly fifty vessels made regular stops at Cleveland with passengers and freight. It was not unusual for a visitor by the late 1830s to see the lake and harbor filled with sail- and steamboats waiting for their turn at the docks and regularly emptying large numbers of immigrants into the town. Without doubt, by the mid-1840s, Cleveland joined Detroit and Buffalo as the dominant Great Lakes ports.

The dramatic increase in trade brought with it good news for the entire village and led to a period of speculative excitement. By 1830, Cleveland had 138 dwellings, 13 stores, and 15 warehouses as the banks along the river became the wholesale district. To complement

Supported by the benefits of being a terminus of the Ohio & Erie Canal, Cleveland had grown into a substantial village by 1832, as shown by this view of the town looking west from Public Square. The Western Reserve Historical Society.

the progress along the river, retail stores located along Superior indicated the beginnings of a central business district. A residential neighborhood also emerged, between Superior and the lake and Ontario and the river. Here early schools and the first church building, Trinity Church, were built. Architecturally, the village was a mix of log cabins, small frame houses, and several more-contemporary buildings, with few traces of its primitive frontier beginnings. During the early 1830s, a series of real-estate schemes developed to exploit interest in tracts on both sides of the river. The floodplain on the west side was poorly drained land that had not been farmed. It was purchased by a group of Buffalo investors hoping northern Ohio would expand as Buffalo had done because of the Erie Canal. The marshlands were drained, and an elaborate hotel was built on the newly surveyed lands. Another scheme involved the development of the oxbow area of the river, which was named Willeyville and laid out in a pattern of radiating streets off a central circle. A bridge built by the investors connected it to the west side. In addition, a planned residential neighborhood, Clinton Square, located just beyond the city limits near the shore, had a central square and a goal of preserving the privacy of residents. All of these ventures temporarily raised land costs in the area, and a number of local investors did benefit. For instance, in March 1835, a tavern located on the west bank changed hands at a profit of $3,000 in one day. Few investors received similar windfalls, however, since these ventures failed because of national economic developments. The real impact of these speculations was to raise land prices during the mid-1830s higher than they would be for the next thirty years.

While some did make money, it was only temporary in most cases. Not all the economic news during the thirties was positive. The Panic of 1837 and the depression that followed stopped much development in the village and stifled economic advance for six or seven years. Cyclical economic downturns had had little impact before the canal brought national markets and national problems to northern Ohio, but now the impact was widespread. William Case noted that, from 1838 to 1840, "speculations ceased—and failures commenced—property about the city fell one half and generally much of it two thirds in

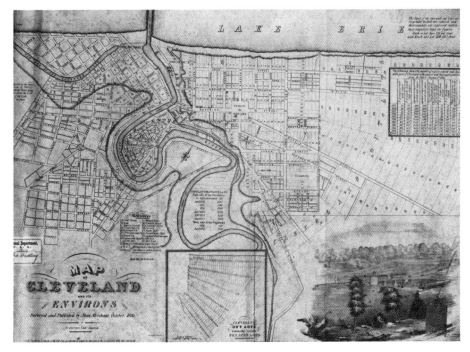

Ahaz Merchant's map of 1835 shows Cleveland just one year before its incorporation as a city. The Western Reserve Historical Society.

value." Banks failed, forcing local stores to produce their own currency, called shinplasters, which were not redeemable universally. These and other economic reversals doomed the dreams of many railroad companies that had been chartered by the state before 1836. Had it not been for the panic, railroad development would have been much quicker, and the era of the canal proportionately shorter. The hard times forced many new residents to leave town in search of work and housing. Also, many cultural institutions formed in the early 1830s disbanded, unable to collect dues from their membership. Only gradually did the country and Cleveland emerge from the depression by 1845.

The panic not only ruined speculation, it also arrested a population spurt that had begun with canal construction in 1826. The village grew from 500 to over 5,000 in the twelve years after 1825, and the west bank of the river added another 1,000 persons. The greatest jump happened between 1833 and 1835, when more than 50 percent of the total arrived. Through 1836, immigrants poured into the village, and Cleveland and its smaller cross-river rival, Ohio City, were named cities in 1836 (even though by modern standards Cleveland was more accurately a town and Ohio City a village). The panic began to limit growth almost immediately. By 1840, 7,500 people lived at the mouth of the Cuyahoga, an increase of only 1,500 in three years—half that of the previous three years. Nevertheless, Cleveland's annual growth made it the fastest-growing city above 1,000 in the state. It continued to grow gradually until, in 1845, 12,000 lived on both banks. Cuyahoga, led by the growing towns, became the most populous county in the Reserve by 1840.

Many migrants settled in the area because of the opportunities offered by local commercial and manufacturing concerns, just as migrants had done before the canal era. The proportion of the population involved in commerce grew, so that in 1840 over 70 percent lived along the river at the lake. More and more workers were involved in small manufacturing establishments, which dotted the two towns. A relatively large number, over one hundred, worked on the west side at the Cuyahoga Steam Furnace Company, the first and, for many years, the only heavy industry of importance in the Cuyahoga Valley. The firm, located on the west side partially because the east bank was crowded with warehouses, became the first of a majority of manufacturing companies established on the west side. Many workers employed by the Steam Furnace Company arrived in the mid-thirties. Some were immigrants from Europe, but most were natives; foreign immigration had just begun. The trend established in the late precanal period continued after 1825, as more and more settlers came from New York State, and relatively fewer from Connecticut and the rest of New England. The natives included more members from the middle and upper class, who came with funds to invest in the future prosperity of Cleveland, much as the land speculators did. In 1830, the village was still over-whelmingly (96 percent) native. Apparently, the canal workers, who included a considerable number of Irish, did not settle in Cleveland. European immigrants did come to the area in the 1830s. Newspapers record several self-help organizations serving Irish, Germans, and Scots during the decade. By 1840, it is likely that well over 25 percent of Cleveland household heads were foreign-born.

By late in the decade, signs of xenophobia appeared in Cleveland and Ohio City newspapers. The *Ohio City Argus* stated on 10 August 1837 that "while our attention is diverted to the numerous shiploads of poor Irish that arrive at our ports, we are not unaware of the num-bers of our own unadulterated Anglo-Saxon race that flock from Ger-many." Three years later the *Herald* commented, on 28 March 1840, "The Germans of our city form a highly respectable, enterprising, in-dustrious, and worthy class of population, and every effort of theirs [is] so commendable . . . [and] should be seconded by the able and good." Most readers immediately understood that these positive char-acterizations were not appropriate for most Irish residents. These ob-servations were juxtaposed with a newly heightened awareness of American traditions, especially obvious in the late forties but which appeared in the thirties. Announcements like the one in the *Herald* of 11 November 1839, which read, "All Yankees are reminded that tomorrow is Thanksgiving day in Yankee-land," served to assert Amer-ican and New England traditions in the face of foreign incursions.

Throughout the two decades after 1825, blacks lived and worked in the village. Their numbers were never very large, and they were not isolated residentially. Cleveland newspapers frequently reported activities of local blacks and on occasion lauded their efforts. The com-munity formed a church in 1830 and a school in 1832. In response to the formation of a young men's union in 1839, the *Herald* com-mented on 29 March, "The colored people of this city are not numer-ous, but of the better class of free blacks. They are industrious, peace-able, intelligent, and ambitious of improvement. A school is supported by them"—as was a lecture series and a library. An equally revealing statement was made by a black responding to a racist letter in the 5

In 1871, Cleveland's German population was large and influential enough to erect a triumphal arch on Public Square to celebrate Germany's victory over France in the Franco-Prussian War. The Western Reserve Historical Society.

November 1845 *Herald.* He stated that there were 56 blacks from twenty families who had accumulated property of $55,000 since 1833 and were employed as canal boat owners and as stewards on boats. Without doubt, racism existed in Cleveland, but the city was a reasonably liberal environment for the times, and some blacks prospered there.

The growing population continued to become more and more differentiated as class and neighborhood distinctions grew and old conventions became outmoded. Titles such as Colonel and Esquire, previously reserved for those who had performed "some act, or acquired some deserved reputation," such as justices of the peace and "aged gentlemen," said the *Herald* in 1844, now seemed to be required for "youth who have passed the age of twenty-one, and who know less of laws and customs than of the last fashion of dressing the hair." It would be better to abolish titles of precedence than to use them "wholly without discrimination," the editor concluded. An upper social group existed in Cleveland during this time, and it was virtually all native. Several dress dances or cotillions occurred before 1845 and were attended by the town elite. Major celebrations, especially on Independence Day, were accompanied by speeches and a dinner where local leaders spoke. Signs of opulence appeared in some homes. In the 1830s, architectural design replaced the vernacular forms used previously. A Georgian-style home, the Crittenden house, built by a leading merchant, was completed in 1832 on Public Square. Four years later, a more contemporary style, Greek Revival, began to take hold, and by the end of the thirties it had replaced Georgian. These new homes were brick and stone rather than wood and were much more imposing than earlier residences. While these are some indications of an elite in Cleveland, after 1845 a more conscious upper class emerged as members formed organizations to promote the city and their own particular view of its needs.

In contrast, the poor were increasingly apparent after the opening of the canal. William Case, a leading figure in the village, believed that by 1828, canal construction had "brought a great many irregular—drinking and rowdy persons" to the city and county. Six years later, in the aftermath of a cholera epidemic that attacked the town, the *Whig* on 9 September 1834 said, "The class of persons among which the disease principally raged" was indicated by the fact that "of about one hundred victims . . . fifty-five were buried at the expense of the town." Many of the poor lived in the Flats, the floodplain on either side of the river, "under the hill." Here the thriving economy spawned numerous "groceries," which appeared on every wharf to dispense alcohol. A racecourse established in 1835 encouraged "a flood of imported depravity, strengthened by all the canaille that could be mustered from groceries and other dens of pollution," asserted the *Whig* of 14 October 1835. Although he probably over-stated the situation, Case said the city council had no power to force "suspicious persons" looking for public support to leave the city, so that at the beginning of the panic, "letters had been written to Ireland, England, Germany, that Cleveland took all the poor that came. In the spring of 1838, the poor came in swarms." Of course, many poor in Cleveland were not "black legs" (professional gamblers) or "out-laws," especially as the depression deepened. So obvious was the need that by the end of 1837, and for several years, a group of ladies coordinated efforts to feed and clothe the poor.

Between these two extremes were the working people of the town. Most laborers had problems of their own, which included the scarcity of housing even to rent and exploitation by employers. As the population increased and canal connections brought eastern ideas and people to Cleveland, workers joined their counterparts and formed local unions. As early as 1834, journeymen printers united, and two years later a meeting of carpenters and joiners of both Cleveland and Ohio City demanded a 10-hour working day. The depression affected workers, and many left the town. Those who stayed probably had difficulty finding work. As the financial problems lifted in 1843, mechanics and laborers of both cities protested the return to barter and asserted that they would accept only cash for their services. Moreover, they promised to form a mechanics' and workingmen's society, and, as one of their first acts, they held a parade where 350 workers protested their financial problems. Activity was not limited to these issues. In the early 1840s, a Mechanics' Lyceum was formed, which promoted lectures on topics of interest to workingmen. All of these gatherings demonstrate an awareness among some workers that they had common interests that could best be served by united action.

Virtually all sectors of Cleveland society united in one form or another during the canal era. As population increased, ethnic and racial distinctions appeared, and social differentiation took place, residents were forced to establish institutions in order to express themselves in a city that lacked the homogeneity and harmony of traditional rural society. Moreover, Cleveland became a regional center during this period by forming branches of eastern institutions. In a sense, the canal brought both commodities and ideas. The first secular organizations were imported from the East when canal construction began. Many had a distinctly religious cast and reflected the conservative New England background of their members. A branch of the American Colonization Society, a group devoted to sending blacks to Africa, was formed in 1826. It marked the first appearance of New England conservatism, which limited local response regarding slavery to the antislavery position rather than to more radical abolitionist views. Subsequently, in 1833, an antislavery society appeared to promote these views. Another popular movement, temperance, reached Cleveland in 1830 and continued for many years. As with most voluntary organizations, members tended to be upper-class, and the targets of their attentions tended to be lower-class. Groups were formed that were able to turn Fourth of July celebrations into celebrations of temperance. In 1834, for instance, children assembled from various Sunday schools, marched, and were treated to cakes, crackers, and cold water in an effort to rid the holiday of "rum and gunpowder." Throughout the period, hotels and steamboats were converted to temperance principles. By 1843, Clevelanders joined a national movement to restrict the sale of liquor by the drink or to prohibit liquor sales to individuals who were drunk, but had little success.

National movements devoted to stimulating intellectual activity also prospered in Cleveland in the 1830s. Numerous public debates took place, especially in the winter months, under the auspices of local branches of the lyceum movement, which continued a local tradition founded in the precanal era. As we have seen, mechanics and blacks founded their own versions of this popular format before 1840. Similar groups, such as the Library Association, the Polemic Association, the Cleveland Reading Room, and various young men's unions, provided refuge from the growing anonymity. They were supplemented by musical organizations such as the Cleveland Mendelssohn and Mozart societies. Service groups added to the institutional maze. The Masons continued to be active despite an anti-Masonic movement that forced them out of sight during the late 1820s and much of the 1830s. Other groups, including the International Order of Odd Fellows, began to hold meetings as early as 1841. Another segment of the community formed private military units, such as the Cleveland Grays and the Cleveland Guards. Composed of native-born Americans, they served social and ceremonial functions in addition to their role in any military actions. Just at the end of the period, in 1843, local women who had been active in poor relief through their churches formed the Martha Washington and Dorcas Society to administer to all poor in Cleveland. They were attempting to supplement earlier mutual-aid groups formed to preserve ethnic, racial, religious, or fraternal bonds by Germans, Irish, Manx, blacks, firefighters, and Baptists. These groups supported the temporary poor through a solitary gift to help them weather a difficult time. They made up the bulk of benevolence in the pre-1845 era, and while they continued after that time, other, more far-reaching relief was necessary.

Religious organizations formed quickly as population increased, and tended to be ethnically exclusive. From a beginning of three churches in 1830, the number rose to twelve Protestant congregations by 1845. The most prominent of these was the First Presbyterian Church, known as Old Stone Church, built in 1834 on Public Square. These congregations formed a series of social groups within their organizations, such as Sabbath schools, Bible classes, and "female benevolent societies." Two Protestant churches were exclusively German and had about six hundred communicants by 1845. By far the most significant change was the formation of the first Roman Catholic parish in 1835, which built St. Mary's on the Flats in the oxbow area three years later. By 1845, there were also two Jewish congregations. In all, the city directory estimated that there were over eight thousand members of religious organizations, many of whom made the church the center of their social activity.

Despite the rapid increase in population and in cultural and religious concerns, Cleveland only gradually provided public education for its citizens. John Willey, first mayor of Cleveland, told the city council in 1836: "Our character, our manners, our habits, and our means require an entire change, the introduction of a liberal and well adjusted system of education in our city" to replace private academies. The next year, a public school system began with a board of managers. After a shaky beginning, the system built three schoolhouses and was firmly established by 1845. Higher education began near the end of the period, when the Cleveland Medical College opened in 1843. The college immediately became successful and was viewed as one of the chief assets of the city. Other, similar institutions came only after 1845, when population and educational trends warranted expansion.

Just as the school system evolved over the two decades, so also politics and city government changed dramatically. Clevelanders not only joined national movements such as temperance and antislavery, they also participated in national politics. The stylistic change to mass appeal and party politics, which had not existed in earlier years, was exemplified by a convention of 15,000 Western Reserve and northern Ohio Whigs who met in Cleveland in October 1844 to ratify Clay's presidential nomination. The evolution that led to this system began as early as 1827, when the first convention was held to determine local candidates. The political preferences of Cleveland's residents betrayed their New England heritage; by and large they were for Clay and the American System of internal improvements beginning in the early twenties, and they consistently opposed Andrew Jackson to the point that no Jacksonian newspaper could survive in the city. In the mid-1830s they remained Whig, and they supported Harrison's campaign in 1840 with great enthusiasm, as they did Clay's in 1844. Newspapers became more and more partisan during the era, and much of their news emphasized political issues. There were also significant changes in local political activity, where "caucusses" that nominated approved candidates were necessary "for the common good," according to the *Herald* on 9 September 1835. Local party representatives established vigilance committees to police voting at each polling place and "to use all honorable means to secure the election of the candidates nominated." Not all means were honorable, however; in 1843, three persons convicted of voting more than once at the spring election were each sentenced to one year in the penitentiary.

All this conscious political activity gradually changed the nature of officeholding during the canal era. It did not, however, change the ethnicity of officers, who remained native despite rising numbers of Germans and Irish in the community. Before 1836, village officers seemed to continue the tradition of public service by serving several years: John W. Allen served four consecutive years as mayor, T. P. May was a trustee for five years, and David Worley served five years as treasurer. After Cleveland became a city, the mayor and city council, consisting of a president, three aldermen, and three councilmen from each of the three wards, formed the government. Over the next nine years, there was no consistent pattern of officeholding. No officer served as mayor, alderman, or councilman more than two years, for instance. Perhaps a writer to the *Herald* on 25 August 1837 correctly observed that Cleveland had "a central aristocracy composed of capitalists, [paper mill owners], and speculators" that shared offices among its members. A brief analysis of these men shows that virtually all were wealthy businessmen, and many were deeply involved in the land speculations of the mid-1830s. Apparently long-term officers were not needed, since the increasing population brought many qualified men to the city. In any case, local leaders did begin to affiliate with political parties, according to Cleveland newspapers. In 1844, the *Herald* suggested that since local Democrats and Whigs had each nominated a candidate for mayor, and since both were old residents, well qualified, and popular, the election of either would be good for the city. Later the same year, the newspaper put the local election into perspective when it stated that the Democrats had won the mayoralty by 32 out of 1,100 votes cast, but the spoils belonged to the Whigs, who held nine of the twelve council seats. The paper continued that over the last four years, these mayoral elections had been so close that the Whigs had won by only 14 votes in 1841, and then the Democrats won by margins of 12, 45, and 32 votes. Politics in the city were partisan, it seems, but the rival factions were drawn from the same ruling group before 1845.

These city leaders had a difficult task managing the transition from village to town over the two decades from 1815 to 1836. As a village with few regulations and few responsibilities, Cleveland had relied on private institutions to provide needed services. Beginning in the late 1820s, Cleveland was forced to regulate more generally and to control more city services itself. Fire protection began in 1829 when the village bought a fire engine and volunteers formed a fire department. By 1836, there were four firehouses, manned by volunteers, and a fire warden examined houses to enforce ordinances designed to prevent fires. As crime increased, the village appointed a marshal in 1832 and four years later formed a city watch, including eight companies of men. Also during this time, the city regulated markets and attempted to centralize them. The condition of city streets was a continuing problem. Repairing dirt roads improved mobility but was not a permanent solution to growing transportation problems. All of these concerns would force more permanent solutions on the city in the years after 1845, but before then only a piecemeal approach was used.

Just as efforts to provide city services did not keep pace with growing demands during the canal era, efforts to create a unified city on both sides of the river were stymied as well. That part of Brooklyn Township directly across the river grew quickly after 1830, and in the winter of 1835 a letter to the *Whig* stated: "I cannot see any good and sufficient reasons why Brooklyn should not be included in the proposed corporation [of Cleveland]. The interests of one place are closely connected and allied with the interests of the other." On 30 December, a Cleveland meeting rejected including the west side, because Clevelanders did not want the opposite bank to benefit from the larger population and tax base of the east side, and because residents feared the influence it would give Brooklyn, Buffalo, and New York speculators. The rejection erupted into a year-long confrontation rooted in the view that each city was fighting for the same business. The immediate issue was the repair or replacement of a floating bridge, but by June 1836, Cleveland removed the bridge because it obstructed navigation. A replacement, the Columbus Street Bridge, was built on the southern edge of Ohio City, diverting traffic to Cleveland rather than letting it pass through Ohio City's business district. In response Ohio City drove piles on the Cleveland side of the river for a new bridge, which caused east-side leaders to order the project halted. After several incidents of vandalism to the new bridge, attributed to unhappy Ohio City residents, a skirmish took place on 31 October 1836 when an attempt was made to saw through its timbers. The bridge's destruction was prevented by Cleveland citizens reinforced by the county sheriff, but according to an Ohio City paper describing the event, the mob began to destroy the structure only after they were fired upon. Subsequently, each village established a watch to protect bridges and buildings. The controversy receded after a year but left scars so deep that any discussion of unification ceased for more than a decade.

These unsettled problems did not obscure Cleveland's progress from 1825 to 1845. A newspaper commented: "But a few short years have passed since our thriving town, (then a rude hamlet) stood upon the farther confines of the rising west. . . . Ours is no longer a western settlement, our children are surrounded by the comforts, the blessings, and the elegance of life." Within these two decades, a village had become a commercial town, thus justifying the foresight of its founders. Cleveland had become the capital of the Reserve. The town had expanded to over 12,000 people and was on the verge of becoming a genuine city. It was also on the verge of several major changes that would make canals obsolete and would require more creative solutions to urban problems. During the next fifteen years, ethnic consciousness increased, and the celebration of Yankee heritage grew markedly as Clevelanders coped with the final phase of the antebellum period.

A National Urban Center Emerges

1845–1860

From 1845 to 1860, Cleveland became a city. Economically, railroads revolutionized transportation, eliminating the need for canals and laying the groundwork for the transition from commerce to manufacturing. Moreover, the city joined other Great Lakes ports in promoting regional economic development. Culturally, Cleveland shed its provincial perspective to become an integral if somewhat conservative part of national trends. Local politics, too, became embroiled in national issues. Significantly, Ohio City and Cleveland united, following the trend of urban annexation. Finally, on the eve of the Civil War, some Clevelanders began to record the proud history of their progress. The economy continued to be the driving force of change during these years, as canal expansion and railroad construction led all other developments. After 1840, feeder lines connecting the canal with Erie, Pennsylvania, the Mahoning Valley, Pittsburgh, and Marietta on the Ohio River ended the monopoly of the Ohio Canal's north-south trunk line as they provided alternate routes and commercial centers. These canals affected Cleveland in much the same way railroads would in the 1850s, for they strengthened its hold on certain commodities, such as grain, while they reduced traffic in other goods, such as foodstuffs. The Mahoning Canal was particularly important for Cleveland, since it opened a direct route to the interior of the Western Reserve and to the Mahoning Valley that funneled dairy products, wool, and coal to the city.

From 1845 to 1852, canals recovered from several poor years in the mid-1840s and canal traffic reached its peak; at the same time, railroads finally attracted enough funds to begin construction. In 1851, the canal brought 2.5 million bushels of wheat, nearly 1 million bushels of corn, .66 million barrels of flour, and 3 million bushels of coal to Cleveland, breaking records for each commodity. The *Herald* of 20 February 1849 praised the long-term impact of the canal, saying that it had "made Cleveland," because while it had cost $5 million to build, it had paid back twenty times that much. Also, the paper estimated that without the canal the village population would have been 3,000 rather than 21,000, and its property worth only $3 million rather than $10 million. Few doubted the evaluation, and few predicted the reversal that followed. In the nine years 1851–1860, flour volume fell by one-third, wheat by well over one-half, and corn by three-fourths: the canal era had ended.

Although the end came quickly, prosperity in the 1840s masked the urgent need for railroad financing and meant that Cleveland was almost left out of this next transportation revolution. Fortunately, as canal traffic peaked, the first rail connection was completed. Railroad promotion began in the 1830s and was revitalized in the mid-1840s. An editorial in late 1845 advocated support for a proposal to have the city of Cleveland purchase $2 million in stock of the Cleveland, Columbus & Cincinnati Railroad and added, "It has become a matter of surprise to our neighbors that Cleveland has been so stupid upon the project of this and other railroads." A letter to the editor of the *Herald* on 14 July 1846 argued that many businessmen and active young men left the city each year to settle in younger cities and towns along the lakes, such as Sandusky, presumably, which had built several railroads because it had no canal connections to the interior. Advocates of trains constantly pointed out that Clevelanders were active only two-thirds of the year; for the other four months, "they burrow like animals." The iron horse, they argued, would initiate a year-round city. Finally, after several ill-organized attempts, the most promising line, the

Cleveland, Columbus & Cincinnati (CC&C), was funded. Construction proceeded quickly, and by early 1851 plans for a celebration marking the arrival of the first train were quickly completed. By year's end, Cleveland was also connected with Painesville and Pittsburgh, and, by 1853, with New York City, Chicago, and St. Louis. On the eve of the Civil War, Cleveland had become one of the major rail centers in the country.

The railroads revived Cleveland. While shipments of manufactured goods on the canal had declined since 1839, rail shipments in 1851 exceeded eleven thousand tons and continued to grow, tripling by 1860. Passenger traffic via canal all but ceased by the end of 1851, as more than sixty-four thousand passengers rode the CC&C. Railroad connections meant that farmers in the Reserve could market their products for twice prerail prices. Small towns increased in size and wealth. Lake traffic benefited by new piers and depots to handle the rise in business volume.

Commerce enhanced prosperity in Cleveland, but some observers saw problems unless the city's economic base broadened. Cleveland was a good place to live, said the *Leader*, 15 March 1856, but there was "no living spirit of enterprise. . . . No thinking man with capital will stop in the city when we have only our commerce to sustain us. A manufacturing town gives a man of means full scope to his ambition . . . commerce alone cannot save Cleveland, as but few are benefited by it directly. Manufacturing creates a demand for merchandise, mechanical labor, all the necessaries of life, and gives tone to all legitimate business in and around it." Moreover, the city had all the right resources—mechanics, raw materials, places to erect factories, and cheap food prices. Despite these advantages, the paper continued, real-estate prices had declined for over two years, and some quick improvement was needed. Other arguments emphasized the ability to weather economic crises by diversifying and the benefit of wresting retail markets in the hinterland away from eastern manufacturers. Manufacturing did exist in the area, and had ever since the founding of the Cuyahoga Steam Furnace Company in the early 1830s. But as the 1853 city directory observed, investment in industry for a city of 33,000 people was much too small given "the capabilities

The Union Depot, Cleveland's second railroad terminal, was completed in 1866 and stood on the lakefront near the foot of what is now West 9th Street. This view was taken shortly after the structure's completion. The Western Reserve Historical Society.

of this location for sustaining manufactures." Most of the 150 establishments added between 1850 and 1860 were small and not related to the nascent iron and oil industries. Instead, they grew because the expanding population needed agricultural implements, woodenware, furniture, clothing, and sewing machines. Although the number of inhabitants who worked in these factories continued to grow, they made up only 9 percent of the workforce on the eve of the Civil War. Iron manufacturing was still in its infancy as the first rolling mills began to produce in the 1850s, and the opening of the mineral resources of Lake Superior had only just begun to have an impact on the forest city by 1860.

Both commerce and manufacturing attracted people to the Cleveland area from 1845 to 1860. Fueled by canal expansion, the city's population jumped by 11,000, practically doubling in the first five years, and tripling the 7,000 residents of 1840. The excitement generated by the completion of the CC&C railroad generated another burst,

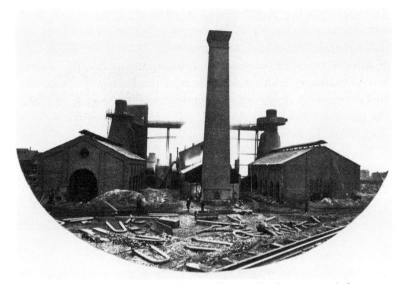

This picture of the Cleveland Rolling Mills shows one of the company's blast furnaces some twenty years after the mills' establishment in 1857. The Western Reserve Historical Society.

which added 8,000 between 1850 and 1853. In all, the population increased by 30,000 to nearly 44,000 at the end of the fifteen years, to lead all cities of comparable size in the country with a 10 percent annual growth rate. Other cities in northeast Ohio grew slowly from 1850 to 1860 in comparison: Akron added several hundred, Canton 2,400, and Warren 1,700. These increases, while not equivalent to that in Cleveland, were the beginning of a significant rural-to-urban movement as the proportion of urban residents in the Western Reserve rose. Clearly these changes suggest the continuing trend toward greater population concentrations. Another continuing trend was the rising proportion of foreign-born immigrating to Cleveland. At mid-century, the native-born made up only one-third of household heads in Cleveland and only two-fifths of those in Ohio City. A decade later, both sides of the river were less than 30 percent native, while 33 percent were German-born and 22 percent were Irish-born residents.

This native minority benefited from the influx of Europeans, who held occupations at the lower end of the economic ladder. Natives filled virtually all skilled positions, such as machinists and shipwrights, as well as more white-collar occupations, including merchants, physicians, and boatbuilders. Irish residents were at the bottom of the ladder. Half, who had no steady employment, were listed as day laborers, and the remainder had semiskilled jobs, such as shoemakers and sailors. Virtually no Irishmen held white-collar jobs. In contrast, 25 percent of the Germans were skilled craftsmen, and many semiskilled Germans worked in the more dependable building trades rather than in the seasonal work along the wharves, as did the Irish.

Economic differences and preference concentrated the various ethnic divisions more and more in their own areas of the city. On the "West Side," for instance, the Irish began to dominate the lowlands near the river and the hillside leading to the heights, where many natives lived in the fashionable Franklin Circle area. Germans made up less than one-fifth of the West Side, except in a new residential area away from the lake south of Bridge Street, where they constituted two-thirds of the households in 1860. These concentrations had their "East Side" equivalents but should not be viewed as ghettos, since many residents were not forced into them by discrimination but chose to live close to countrymen. However, the increased presence of foreign-born undoubtedly raised ethnic consciousness in the city. A newspaper editorial on 18 February 1851 offered a formula of assimilation that few followed when it advised foreigners to immediately become "Americanized" by "casting off" their European skins and encouraged natives to welcome them as brothers. Throughout the period, ethnic groups, especially Germans, created numerous organizations to preserve their languages and cultures and continued the self-help groups formed in the 1830s. Germans added a German-language newspaper in 1846, a military group, the German Guards, in 1847, and a German music society in 1848. In the 1850s, many *Saengerbunden*, German singing societies, were formed, and in 1859 the city hosted a North American *Saengerfest*, which included a group of four hundred singers from Cleveland representing twenty-four separate local societies. Local churches expanded, as well, and by 1860 there were six German congregations. Some attempts to preserve culture were not successful, especially when they seemed to oppose Americanization. The Ohio City Council denied a request for the formation of a separate German school in 1853, for instance, but it did agree to print in both English and German a city ordinance regulating dogs.

Other ethnic groups did not form as many private organizations. Irish residents relied on churches and schools for their cultural activities, although there were also organizations such as the Hibernerian Guards and the Irish Naturalization Society of Cleveland. By 1860, there were four churches and seven parochial schools in the city. Throughout the period, there was little mention of the Irish in the newspapers. A great deal is made of the formation of the Father Mathew Total Abstinence Society in 1851, which brought many Catholics into an essentially Protestant movement and promised an end to the heavy-drinking Irish stereotype that pervaded Cleveland newspapers. By 1853, the problem had not yet been completely solved, as the *Herald* of 9 January publicized the "low bacchanalean orgies" which took place "at an Irish hovel near the corner of Roots alley and the lake shore." Immigrants from Scotland and the Isle of Man, who did not receive such negative characterizations, formed self-help organizations and were able to report in 1856 that only one countryman from each group had ever received city aid.

Blacks, too, increased in numbers and continued to associate in organizations for their social and economic improvement. They never made up more than 2 percent of the population, and they were not isolated residentially. Blacks worked at many levels of the occupational scale: 35 percent were unskilled; 45 percent were skilled; and 20 percent were semiskilled. Of course, serious questions of racism concerned all blacks. Three meetings held in Cleveland in 1847 considered a petition to Congress asking for enough land in a western area for blacks to form their own government and send representatives to Congress, but rejected it because slaveholders controlled the legislature. Several churches created new opportunities for religious and social activities, as did the Colored Young Men's Union Society, a debating club, and the Colored Association of Cleveland. The plight of blacks was explicitly highlighted by a newspaper, the *Aliened American*, published in 1853. The court system seemed to treat blacks with some fairness; a white in 1849 was found guilty of killing a black and was sentenced for the crime, while in 1854 a black man charged with raping a white girl was freed after it was learned she "did not sustain a good character."

The local upper class had formed a tight-knit society that entertained itself and attempted to control the destiny of the city. After 1845, when Cleveland became a boom town, one could have measured the social and cultural evolution of the upper class, because they began to copy eastern styles as quickly as they appeared in the East. By the late 1840s, Gothic houses had begun to replace earlier Greek Revival styles, and architectural provincialism had all but disappeared as eastern architects brought the latest fashion to Cleveland. A decade later, Italian villa designs, such as the one built by Amasa Stone, appeared along the posh section of Euclid Avenue. Stone's home featured rosewood and mahogany highlights and a heating system with a fireproof furnace that sent heated water to nearly every room. The house was the finest in the city.

The Protestant upper class did become more physically separated from the growing congestion of the central city, but, at the same time, it also became more concerned with benevolence. What had been the purview of a few devoted wealthy women and ethnic self-help groups became an effort of prominent male leaders to instill the values of their heritage, especially self-discipline and Protestant morality, into the poor. Moreover, these leaders turned the attention of private and public organizations more toward the idle and begging class than to newly arrived immigrants or the ill. In so doing, they forged a movement that wished not only to help but also to control, as much out of fear as out of concern, and as further evidence of a growing class consciousness. There was legitimate reason for concern. The number of poor increased as the city population increased and as the cyclical downturns in the economy forced more newcomers out of work. Poor relief was a real problem, and when unemployment increased in 1856, the city provided outdoor relief. A survey of the beneficiaries concluded that 47 percent were Irish, 22 percent German, and only 12.5 percent

"Americans." Throughout the 1850s, while the local economy weathered the panics reasonably well, each downturn reduced the number of workers dramatically, thereby increasing the number of needy. The majority of city residents fell between these two extremes. The working population continued to form groups to protect its interests during the late 1840s and the 1850s. Cleveland's garment industry employed mostly women, and they protested against low wages and bad treatment in 1848 and formed a sewing society twenty years later. For a short time they ran their own shop. Throughout the 1850s, economic problems increased union activity. Most workingmen settled in areas where they could afford housing. On the West Side, housing costs dropped after the speculative boom of the thirties, and prices stayed low so that, in contrast to Cleveland, separate houses were available to most people, and "nearly all had breathing room." Further opportunities meant that a large number of "men of small means" could buy lots on the West Side, build houses there, and be nearer to work than those who had to live on the East Side. Less-affluent laborers and workers clustered around Lorain Avenue and south and west of Pearl. Consequently, financial considerations, along with ethnic loyalties and xenophobia, created residential segregation by the end of the antebellum period.

A great variety of private and public institutions were founded between 1845 and 1860 to accommodate the growing complexities of city life within a national cultural context. Some organizations, such as antislavery or temperance societies, expanded their activities and involved more than local residents. In Cleveland, church leaders from congregational and Presbyterian churches dominated the abolition affiliates. While Cleveland was not a hotbed of abolitionism even in the 1850s, it was a stop for a few prominent abolitionist lecturers, including Frederick Douglass and Cassius Clay. Two related shortcomings of the city that kept it from more radical ideas and, in part, reflected its general propensities were the absence of an abolitionist press and the conservative editorial policies of the city's daily newspapers. More in keeping with its conservative New England heritage was local support for antislavery. Throughout the 1850s, some runaway slaves were helped, mostly through the efforts of local blacks, and occasionally by whites. Such actions were illegal, according to the Fugitive Slave Act of 1850, but many Clevelanders were proud of their defiance. The most dramatic indication of local sentiments was the excitement generated by the Oberlin-Wellington rescue and fugitive slave trial, when thirty-seven rescuers were jailed. Throughout the proceedings, which took place in Cleveland, crowds gathered, and at one rally ten thousand attended. At the same time, soon-to-be-martyred John Brown, then a fugitive because of his actions in Kansas, stayed in the city. When he was hanged for his role at Harpers Ferry, flags flew at half-mast and bells tolled in Cleveland, partially because he represented courage and freedom in spite of his unacceptable methods.

In politics, local business leaders tried to replace Representative Joshua R. Giddings with a candidate of more moderate views on slavery but failed and were forced to rely on him. Throughout the 1840s, Clevelanders supported antislavery Whigs, but in the 1850s they joined the movement led by Giddings and others through the successive stages of antislavery parties from Free-Soil to the Whig-Free-Soil-Independent Democratic party, known as the Republicans. So while local leaders and voters were reluctant followers of this limited national shift, they joined the organizations and were committed by the eve of the war. The temperance movement in Cleveland followed a similar path, as it too became involved in politics. The Washingtonians, a group prominent in the 1840s, expanded the temperance cause and paved the way for the Sons of Temperance and the Independent Order of Good Templars. Both of these fraternal organizations offered fellowship and social events but were primarily devoted to protecting their members from drink and to elevating their politics. Gradually, in the 1850s, they became more active in politics. In 1853, they could not obtain a temperance position from either major gubernatorial candidate, so the Cleveland Temperance Alliance supported a Free-Soil Democrat. As we have seen, there were also Catholic temperance groups formed after the 1851 visit of Father Mathew, a protemperance priest. The numerous groups often offered direct aid to countrymen and participated in Fourth of July parades to counteract the portrayal of intemperance among immigrants.

Private relief groups also sought to aid the poor in more systematic ways. The Society for the Relief of the Poor, formed in 1850, and its successor, the Relief Association, as well as the Sons of Malta, were upper-class, male-dominated groups that gave aid to those poor who were deserving because of their moral character and potential for improvement. Typical of the terms of relief were the stipulations of the City Mission of the Euclid Street Presbyterian Church, which stated that "no continued or permanent relief [would] be granted any family . . . not . . . connected with some Protestant [congregation]" and that relief recipients would be subject to periodic visitations to determine whether they were worthy of help. By the mid-1850s, leaders of these groups realized that they did not have the resources to deal with the problem and consequently began a campaign to have the government assume more responsibility. Uncared-for children created another problem, which church groups helped solve with the formation of the Protestant Orphan Asylum and similar Catholic institutions in the early 1850s. In addition, the Ragged School was founded to attract children too poor to attend public schools. Some of these institutions, especially the Ragged School, were partially or totally funded by the city after private efforts proved insufficient.

Not all voluntary groups sought to solve urban problems; some sought to improve the social and intellectual environment of their members. German music groups proliferated in the period, and in 1854 the Cleveland Academy of Music, a theater, opened. From the foundation laid in the 1830s and partially destroyed by the depression of the 1840s, the Cleveland Library Association revived and by mid-century had a collection of more than two thousand volumes. Moreover, business leaders who were involved in church groups and other benevolent societies in the Cleveland area also formed a Board of Trade where they could discuss economic issues and meet peers. Fraternal associations such as the Masons and Odd Fellows met throughout the period. Social and athletic clubs such as the Ivanhoe Boat Club, the Cleveland Cricket Club, the Cleveland Chess Club, and local gymnasium groups all prospered during the period. Sports activities and public celebrations increased markedly in the 1850s. Horseracing revived and became an annual event, drawing as many as three thousand people. Footraces and baseball also took place. By far the most popular celebration occurred annually on the Fourth of July; it attracted forty thousand people in 1858. Residents also had opportunities to attend countless musical concerts and plays. In 1853, a theatrical rendition of *Uncle Tom's Cabin* played to twelve thousand people in fifteen performances.

Churches grew rapidly as they attracted new communicants. The number of Protestant congregations nearly tripled over the course of the fifteen years, to thirty-four in 1860, and they supported thirty-eight Sunday schools. Just as the social order became more differentiated, so too did local churches. Some church leaders were members of the local upper class who built new church buildings reflecting their own stature, and others took an active role in the political issues that permeated all levels of society. Churches after 1845 followed Gothic and Romanesque designs imported directly from the East. Political and moral beliefs were inevitably enmeshed in the antebellum period, and some local congregations felt the effects. In March 1850, Presbyterians who favored abolition formed their own church. Catholic churches continued to expand, so that in 1860 there were four separate churches, whose congregations supported several orphan asylums and four parochial schools, including a seminary.

The realization that private institutions could no longer handle many urban social problems caused city government to take over some institutions founded by voluntary associations and to create others. The city poorhouse had served few poor in the late 1830s and 1840s, since private groups provided considerable aid; but as the problem increased, a Poorhouse & Hospital was built to house the sick, the insane, the indigent, and the aged poor. The City Infirmary could minister only to meritorious cases who had been residents for at least one year. In 1857, the Ragged School, which had been founded by private groups, was taken over by the city. Its goal was to change "scholars from dangerous to industrious citizens." The city also saw the need for expanded educational opportunities for all residents. From 1846 to 1860, the number of school buildings rose from thirteen to seventeen, and the number of students from fifteen hundred to six thousand. A Board of Education, formed in 1853, directed the system. In addition to the Ragged School, renamed the Industrial School in 1857, which trained poor youth, a high school opened in 1846 that trained those who wanted to learn the higher branches of education; and a night school opened in 1850 to aid those who needed to work but wished to learn as well. In all, public education had virtually replaced private education on the eve of the Civil War; only three secular schools remained in Cleveland in 1860, whereas a quarter-century before, nearly all pupils had attended private academies.

Other city services increased to meet the demands of the growing population. One obvious sign of the number of newcomers was an 1848 city ordinance placing street signs at various corners. Public utilities were also in demand. Water from wells supplied homes, but the business district needed a larger amount, which was provided when a large holding tank was constructed in 1849. It proved insufficient, so by 1856 a system was built that pumped lake water to the Kentucky Street Reservoir on the West Side and then distributed it. Gas lighting was introduced to downtown streets and buildings in 1850 and gradually spread south and east from Public Square, along the main streets going east, and to the West Side by 1857. Streets continued to be a problem throughout the period, as surfaces constantly needed repair and as a primitive sewage system designed to drain main streets proved inadequate. Partially because of this problem as well as crowded housing, the city appointed a public health officer in 1856 and formed a board of health as a permanent structure, which replaced earlier boards created to deal with specific emergencies. Fire and police protection kept pace with other changes. Cleveland had ten fire engines and a volunteer group of five hundred firemen to cope with the growing number of fires. Police protection expanded as the small watch forces of the 1830s were replaced by a formal police department that employed forty patrolmen by 1860. More local station houses appeared in immigrant communities and other areas where crime was more prevalent. The justice system also expanded to meet new demands, as a police court was formed in 1853. In addition, a federal district court was established in Cleveland in 1855 as a result of the increasing financial position of the city.

All of these new services sought to make living and working better in the new city. The long, difficult period of contention between

This late nineteenth-century view shows the officers of one of the many police stations established throughout the growing city following the establishment of a police department in 1866. The Western Reserve Historical Society.

Cleveland and Ohio City ended when they united in 1854. The two had cooperated on bridge and harbor projects in the 1840s, which initiated attempts to unite them in the early 1850s. The reasons for unification were obvious: the river would be under one authority; the harbor would receive federal money more easily; property values, especially of Ohio City lots close to the Flats, would increase; and administration would be streamlined. Nevertheless, while 88 percent of Ohio City voters wanted union, Clevelanders rallied in an antiunion assault and rejected the proposal in 1851. Three years later, the issue returned with new benefits. New taxes, increased real-estate values for the East Side business district, access to "fresh, pure water" from the West Side's system, and the addition of the industrial capacity of "manufactories, iron works, machine shops, and warehouses" apparently convinced Clevelanders, who voted 4 to 1 in favor of union. Ohio City voters also approved annexation. The terms of the 1854 merger created four West Side wards and guaranteed that a bridge joining the two banks would be built within two years, but also ensured West Side dependence by reserving the revenues and assets of each before the union to that side exclusively. Cleveland benefited immediately because Ohio City brought a commitment to manufacturing and helped turn the new city away from commerce.

Local politics became more complex after the union, since more local offices were available as the number of wards reached eleven and the office of alderman was abolished. Just as religious and secular organizations became involved in national politics, so too did local elections. In the canal era, there was a constant turnover of officeholders as the pool of available men grew; after 1848, however, officers often served more than two years, probably because of the rising effectiveness of local parties. Their new tactics included efforts to muster German and Irish voters, beginning in 1852. Three years later, the *Daily True Democrat* reported on 15 May a rather strong reversal of this approach, and one that was in concert with a national native-born-American political movement, the Know-Nothing party. The paper reported that a crowd of "jackasses and hyenas and bawdy house bullies" had taken over the polls in the First and Second wards, refusing to allow any anti-Know-Nothing foreigner to approach. All Germans were kept from voting and were beaten if they attempted to come too near. Whether these tactics continued is not known, but the Democratic party won nearly all the municipal offices in 1856. Clearly, local politics had become more organized and effective in the prewar years. Local connections to national parties were important as the rather conservative political views of many residents gradually joined the national trend to the left. Through the 1850s, Clevelanders supported Franklin Pierce over Winfield Scott in 1852, Fremont over Buchanan in 1856, and finally Lincoln in 1860. This shift toward the Republican coalition placed the area in the mainstream of American politics, just as it had gradually joined the economic and cultural mainstreams by the close of the antebellum period.

By 1860, Cleveland was one of the most beautiful cities in the country, with all the potential associated with urban centers. It had matured quickly, even by nineteenth-century standards. When the *Herald* compared the first city directory, published in 1837, to the one twenty years later, it saw major changes. Travel to Cincinnati had taken eighty hours by canal in 1837 but took only ten in 1857. The number of names in the directory had increased from thirteen hundred to eleven thousand while the number of factory workers had grown from two hundred to three thousand. Other, more subtle differences included the growing separation of the city into a wholesale and commercial zone, a central business district, and numerous residential neighborhoods distinguished from one another by the quality of the houses and the spacing between them. This differentiation was not only economic but also social and cultural, as various institutions with

James A. Garfield, twentieth president of the United States, was born on a farm in Orange Township. He was one of the nationally prominent figures to emerge from the Western Reserve during the Civil War era. The Western Reserve Historical Society.

distinctly ethnic identities replaced the informal relationships of the precanal era. In effect, the social spectrum had widened, and organizations reflected this broadening. Efforts to preserve traditional values through cultural associations became increasingly popular as many groups, especially natives, felt threatened by the majority foreign-born population. Conservative easterners had found ways to preserve their values by cultural associations and by joining national movements with a conservative bent. They also were able to form a ruling group that controlled the local economy and local politics. Urban problems and governmental solutions signaled the end of the era of voluntary associations providing most of the social services to the community. In spite of all its problems, however, Cleveland in 1860 was a fully developed city with a brilliant economic future and a population capable of meeting the challenges it would present.

RW

Part Three

RISE OF THE INDUSTRIAL CITY

CHAPTER SIX

A City Transformed

1860–1869

War and industry governed Cleveland in the 1860s. One fed the other, prompting historian Crisfield Johnson to remark neatly, almost two decades later, "The war found Cleveland a commercial city and left it a manufacturing city." While the Civil War exacted a terrible toll—more than a quarter of the men who served from Cuyahoga County were killed or wounded—its demands for materiel and supplies fueled nascent industries and started the city on the road to industrialization.

Cleveland in 1860 was a small commercial city of just 43,417. The city's boundaries, embracing an area of seven square miles, stretched from Gordon (West 65th) Street on the west to Willson (East 55th) Street on the east. It was a city of merchants, clerks, teamsters, and draymen, a city of small shops, docks, and warehouses. The *Cleveland City Directory for 1859–60* listed more than 40 blacksmiths, 18 hotels, dozens of boarding houses, more than 200 groceries (but only 1 laundry), more than 150 saloons (but only 2 restaurants), scores of carpenters, and 14 "Daguerreans" (photographers). Horse-drawn streetcars ran on Euclid Avenue to Erie (East 9th) Street, turned south to Prospect, then east to the city limits. Lower Superior Street was the center of commerce, and the city's ceremonial center, the gaslit Public

Square, was a "beauty spot"—a proper setting for the statue of Commodore Oliver Hazard Perry erected on 10 September that year, the first monument to grace the town common. But there were unmistakable signs of change.

Railroads had invaded the city, supplementing the numerous canal and steamboat lines already in service. By 1860, five railroad lines were operating in and out of Cleveland. Completion of the Atlantic & Great Western Railroad in 1863, linking Cleveland and New York, provided yet another route to the East and increased the movement of oil and coal from the fields of western Pennsylvania to Cleveland. The Flats (the lowland flanking the river) and the lakefront filled with roundhouses, warehouses, oil tanks, lumberyards, and factories. In 1865, the railroads joined in erecting a new Union Depot at the foot of Water (West 9th) Street to replace a wooden depot burned the previous year. The massive stone station, with a roof supported by iron trusses, was the largest enclosed space in the city.

Early in the decade, newspapers complained about the lack of industrial progress. "Much talk is heard in Cleveland on the subject of manufacturing," the *Cleveland Leader* commented on 10 August 1860, "but nothing much is done about it. We continue to make nothing and buy everything." The economic inertia was short-lived. Cleveland's enviable location on major rail and water routes put it in an ideal position to attract those industries that depended on an abundance of raw materials and ready access to the nation's markets. By the close of the Civil War, there were thirty oil refineries in Cleveland producing kerosene and lubricants. Lake Superior iron ore had first made its way to Cleveland in quantity with the opening of the Sault Sainte Marie Canal in 1855; shipments now increased annually, fueling the city's fledgling iron and steel industry and boosting Cleveland to prominence as an important transshipment point. By 1868, the Board of Trade reported fourteen rolling mills in the Cleveland area. The city's factories were producing machinery, castings, bar iron, nails and spikes, structural iron, railroad equipment, and stoves. The 1870 census reported 1,149 manufacturing establishments in Cuyahoga County, employing just over 10,000 people.

These were the formative years for what would prove to be one of

By the mid-1870s, Cleveland's Flats—the Cuyahoga River Valley—
had evolved into a bustling commercial and industrial center with
grain elevators, lumberyards, and ore docks. The Western Reserve
Historical Society.

the city's important iron and steel enterprises. The Cleveland Rolling
Mill Company (later the American Steel & Wire Division of United
States Steel Corporation) had its origin in the firm of Chisholm, Jones
& Company, founded in 1857. In its earliest years, the company employed 150 men and produced 50 tons of railroad iron daily. When it
was reorganized as the Cleveland Rolling Mill Company in 1863, its
incorporators included some of the city's most influential businessmen. Their biographies are typical of Cleveland's early industrial leaders, who tended to be well-to-do, professionally trained New Englanders or, less frequently, highly skilled immigrant entrepreneurs.

Henry Chisholm, a Scot, had come (by way of Montreal) to Cleveland in 1850 to supervise construction of a breakwater for the Cleve-

land & Pittsburgh Railroad; Andros B. Stone, a Massachusetts native, was a bridge builder and brother of railroad builder and financier Amasa Stone; Stillman Witt, also from Massachusetts, was a railroad builder and manager; Jeptha H. Wade, a native of New York State, was a financier and promoter of the telegraph; and Henry B. Payne, also from New York, was a prominent attorney and politician. By 1866, the Cleveland Rolling Mill Company operated two plants, a steel works at Newburgh and the former Lake Shore Rolling Mill on the lakefront at Wason (East 38th) Street. These plants employed five hundred men, mostly Welsh and Scots, although that number would multiply tenfold in succeeding decades and the company would play a central role in the city's labor history.

The Civil War accelerated the growth not only of industry but also of population. Between 1860 and 1870, the city's population more than doubled, from 43,417 to 92,829. In 1860, the majority of Clevelanders were still transplanted New Englanders and other native stock. But a significant number—45 percent—were foreign-born, the majority from Germany, Ireland, and England. Fifteen Czech families came to the city in 1860, and the first Hungarians and Italians began to arrive in this decade. There were about eight hundred blacks in Cleveland, most of whom lived south of Public Square in the Ontario Street market district. Wealthy citizens, meanwhile, had built fine residences around Public Square and on Superior and Euclid avenues as far as Erie Street. On the West Side, Tremont and Ohio City were closely built with the cottages of artisans and the mansions of mill owners.

Rapid industrial growth and civil war increased the number of sick, poor, and homeless in Cleveland, and myriad private welfare societies were formed to address these problems. In 1867, the evangelical Bethel Union was incorporated for mission work and maintenance of a boardinghouse for sailors and others in need. The following year, the Young Women's Christian Association was founded to aid young women leaving the farm for jobs in the city. Jewish and Catholic orphanages were established in the 1860s, as were several private hospitals, including St. Vincent's Hospital (1865), the city's first permanent general hospital, and the Cleveland City Hospital Society (1866, later University Hospitals of Cleveland). While the Kentucky (West 38th)

Street Reservoir remained a showplace for visitors, the city suffered from poor sanitation, and contagious diseases were common. The Cuyahoga River already had become "a sort of intercepting sewer," according to one observer, and in 1867 the city undertook surveys for construction of a tunnel reaching farther out into the lake to provide more potable water.

There were other signs of the city's growth and increasing complexity. In 1864, the Cleveland City Council passed an ordinance creating a paid fire department. The following year, a council committee was appointed to consider, for the first time, the establishment of public parks. Following passage of the Metropolitan Police Act by the Ohio General Assembly, the Cleveland Police Department was formed in 1866, replacing patrol by a small cadre of constables assisted by volunteer night watchmen. City growth also prompted the expansion of

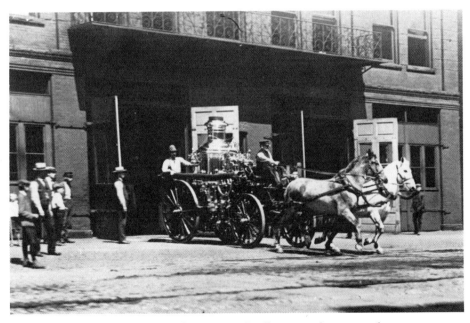

Cleveland's city fire department, officially organized in 1863, depended on horse-drawn apparatus until the early part of the twentieth century. The Western Reserve Historical Society.

public transportation. In 1859, the city council had granted franchises to two companies, the East Cleveland Railway Company and the Woodland Avenue Street Railroad, to lay rails in the streets. Service began in 1860. Between 1863 and 1876, eight other companies were formed to operate horse-drawn railways.

Cleveland, a center of the abolition movement, had voted emphatically for Lincoln in 1860, and the outbreak of war found the city enthusiastic in its support of the Union. When President Abraham Lincoln called for volunteers, Melodeon Hall on Superior Street was filled with patriotic Clevelanders. Within two days the first Cleveland Grays were mustered into service as Company D, the First Ohio Volunteer Infantry. Several months later, a draft was required in three city wards that had not provided sufficient recruits. Except for a period in the winter of 1864 when volunteers waned, support for the war effort remained strong and the conscription riots common to New York never materialized in Cleveland. Camp Cleveland, on University Heights in the Tremont section, was the largest of the city's seven Civil War camps. There, local regiments were organized and trained before

The horse-drawn cars of the Superior Street railway shown in this photograph (about 1880) typified Cleveland's public transportation system until the widespread introduction of electric streetcars in the 1890s. The Western Reserve Historical Society.

being sent into service; they returned to Camp Cleveland for payment and discharge. Many of the wounded were treated at the United States General Hospital, a 320-bed Army hospital erected opposite the camp in 1862.

The war left its mark on the city. About 10,000 men from Cuyahoga County served in the military; some 1,700 died in the war, and 2,000 others were crippled. Those who stayed behind worked to supply wartime demands. The city's factories produced uniforms, knitted goods, railroad iron, and hardware for military use. Cleveland businesses—including John D. Rockefeller's consignment firm, which sold grain, meat, and produce—prospered. Some Clevelanders, meanwhile, worked to alleviate the suffering caused by war, opening soup houses and canvassing for food, clothing, and supplies to assist the needy families of soldiers. The Soldiers' Aid Society of Northern Ohio, an out-

Civil War soldiers mustered on Cleveland's Public Square in 1865. Nearly two-thirds of the 15,600 Cuyahoga County men eligible for service joined or were drafted into the Union Army. The Western Reserve Historical Society.

growth of the Ladies' Aid Society organized by Cleveland women in 1861, provided assistance to Civil War soldiers and veterans until 1868.

During his visit to Cleveland in February 1861, President-elect Lincoln had been greeted by enthusiastic crowds. Little more than four years later, on 28 April 1865, the city was a stopover for the Lincoln funeral train. Amid heavy rain, an estimated 100,000 mourners filed past the slain president, who lay in state beneath a canopied pavilion on Public Square. A saddened nation was in the throes of change, and so was Cleveland.

"Cleveland must rise, if at all, by manufacturing," the *Cleveland Leader* had asserted in 1860. The decade had borne out those words. By the end of the 1860s, there were many who believed that Cleveland had no rival on the Great Lakes. Although the community still retained much of its New England character, by 1870 the impact of industry and immigration was palpable.

CHAPTER SEVEN

The Industrial Age

1870–1899

The Industrial Revolution swept America—and Cleveland—into a new era that would leave both forever changed. Cleveland's transformation from a small, predominantly Yankee commercial city to a large, multiethnic industrial city had a profound impact on the city's economic, social, cultural, political, and intellectual life. Historian James Beaumont Whipple has characterized the period as one of conflict between the Cleveland mind—still deeply rooted in the American (and, especially, Puritan New England) past—and the challenges of a dramatically new social and economic order. That conflict would become apparent as the city grappled with volatile labor problems and growing welfare needs in the coming decades.

In *Cleveland: The Making of a City*, William Ganson Rose vividly described the smell and sound of the age: "The smoke of prosperity mingled with the odor of hemp and canvas, oil, and grease. . . . The air was filled with hoarse blasts from steamship whistles, the clang of ships' bells, and the hoot of tugs and locomotives. Industry was making men rich." There was an aura of recklessness and romance; opportunity abounded in new cities like Cleveland, and in the vigorous new enterprises they spawned. But there was a darker side, too. Immigrants, the critical fuel for the industrial machine, had come seeking a better life; instead, many found themselves trapped by poverty and dehumanizing work. The burgeoning city, meanwhile, found it difficult to cope with unprecedented demands for social and municipal services.

During these years, Cleveland was ruled by a wealthy and close-knit aristocracy that dominated the city's business, civic, and cultural life. They had come to the Western Reserve from Protestant New England; they lived in close proximity in the mansions on Euclid Avenue; they entertained each other; they summered together; they followed the activities of society in the weekly *Cleveland Town Topics*. Mather, Norton, Oglebay, Squire, Brush, Rockefeller, Stone, Hay, Holden, Severance, Hanna: their names were familiar and appeared in newspapers with regularity. In 1904, the reformer Frederic C. Howe would aptly describe Cleveland as "Puritan in its social and ethical consciousness and almost as foreign as Chicago in its ethnic make-up." That duality—a contented, native-born aristocracy on the one hand, and an increasingly heterogeneous, multiethnic city on the other—was a distinctive feature of the city's character.

Cleveland in 1870, with 92,829 people, was now the fifteenth largest city in the nation. With the annexation of portions of Brooklyn and Newburgh townships in 1867, it encompassed 12 square miles and 18 wards. With the annexation of East Cleveland Village in 1872, the city limits pushed eastward, past Doan's Corners. Further expansion came with the annexation of parts of Brooklyn, Newburgh ("the iron ward"), and East Cleveland townships in 1873, and with West Cleveland and Brooklyn villages in 1894. A bird's-eye view of the city in 1877 would reveal the physical pattern still discernible more than a century later: Railroad rights of way followed the most expedient routes (along the lakefront and through the Flats to the old riverbed), while commerce and industry filled the Flats, and warehouses and commercial blocks climbed up Superior Hill and spread northward to the lake. Where pastures had supported cattle in the 1850s, oil refineries and foundries now squatted along the river valley. Homes clustered in a broad arc on the city's plateaus, punctuated by church steeples, while the Cuyahoga River near Lake Erie was a forest of masts. Although Public Square remained a green space, it was now virtually surrounded by commercial blocks, and the first commercial buildings had been erected on Euclid Avenue near the Square—the start of a trend.

Euclid Avenue, between Muirson (East 12th) and Case (East 40th) streets, was known as one of the most beautiful streets in America. Dotted with stately mansions, with arching elms lining the street and graceful fountains set amid impeccably landscaped lawns, Euclid Avenue would remain fashionable through the first decade of the 1900s. Here were the homes of the city's native-born aristocracy: the president and partners of Standard Oil, the developer of the arc light and practical electric power, railroad financiers, shipping and iron ore executives, bankers, and vessel owners. On Cleveland's West Side, large houses with broad lawns lined Franklin Avenue, which came to rival Euclid Avenue as a fashionable address.

Until the expansion of electric streetcars in the 1890s, Cleveland was a "walking" city, with the walking distance between homes and jobs, schools, and stores limiting the reach of settlement. It was compact; the homes of the wealthy stood cheek by jowl with those of mill hands. In *Prologue* (1931), Cleveland playwright Charles S. Brooks recalled growing up on Franklin Avenue in the 1880s in a neighborhood of rambling Victorian mansions. One alley near his own upper-class home, Brooks wrote, "opened to a foreign district where unkempt linen always hung on the line and shrill mothers clamored for their children. . . . Identical tenements were crowded close in foreign sociability—English warped with Irish and with German." Late in the century, the mix of class and ethnic groups that characterized the neighborhoods of nineteenth-century Cleveland would give way to an increasingly stratified city.

The flow of raw materials into and through the city generated a flurry of entrepreneurial activity and provided the foundation for Cleveland's rise as a national industrial center. It spawned huge shipping, materials-handling, and shipbuilding industries. Samuel Livingston Mather's Cleveland Iron Mining Company had pioneered the iron ore trade in the 1850s, and in 1882 his son Samuel formed the rival Pickands, Mather & Company. Both companies operated extensive

Millionaires' Row: Great mansions lined the north side of Euclid Avenue near East 24th Street in 1910. In 1989, only one home shown in this view, that of Samuel Mather, survived, as part of the Cleveland State University campus. The Western Reserve Historical Society.

mines in the Lake Superior district and large fleets of bulk carriers that contributed to Cleveland's dominance of the shipping industry on the Great Lakes. In 1880, Alexander E. Brown, a Scottish immigrant, invented a mechanical hoist that reduced inefficient (and arduous) hand labor and revolutionized ore unloading on the Great Lakes. Cleveland's George H. Hulett patented an even more radical improvement in 1898; the electrically powered Hulett unloader, with its giant clamshell buckets, dramatically reduced labor costs and unloading times and led to larger, specially designed vessels. Captain Alva Bradley, a Connecticut-born seaman, moved his Vermilion, Ohio, shipyard to Cleveland in 1868 and, in the next two decades, built a fleet of eighteen lake vessels and an extensive real-estate empire.

The city gave rise, as well, to one of the nation's most powerful industrialists, John D. Rockefeller. Son of a snake-oil salesman, Rockefeller had come to Cleveland with his family from New York State in 1853. He worked as a bookkeeper for Cleveland commission merchants and established his own commission house before entering the oil business full time in 1865. Rockefeller established a crude-oil refinery at the junction of Kingsbury Run and the Cuyahoga River, and gradually bought out his competitors. By the 1880s, the Standard Oil Company controlled 90 percent of the nation's refining capacity and Rockefeller was one of the richest men in America. Petroleum refining, with its demand for massive quantities of sulphuric acid, attracted pioneer chemist Eugene Grasselli to Cleveland from Cincinnati in 1867; he established the Grasselli Chemical Company to meet the needs of oil refiners, especially Standard Oil, in the Kingsbury Run district.

The growing iron and steel industry had a ripple effect, prompting the formation of important secondary enterprises. The Eberhard Manufacturing Company, for example, founded in 1881, produced

Oil millionaire John D. Rockefeller maintained two homes in Cleveland, one at East 40th Street and Euclid Avenue and this summer home at Forest Hill in what is now East Cleveland. The Cleveland Public Library.

carriage, wagon, and saddlery hardware (and, later, automotive hardware). The Walworth Run Foundry Company produced grey iron castings for furnaces, registers, and stoves. The Van Dorn Iron Works Company, a manufacturer of iron fencing and jail cells, moved from Akron to Cleveland in 1878 and soon diversified into a wide range of iron products, from truck frames to mailboxes. The King Iron Bridge & Manufacturing Company, organized in 1871 by Vermont native Zenas King, was the largest highway bridge works in the United States during the 1880s, employing a network of agents in Boston, Philadelphia, Kansas City, and other large cities. Such enterprises were typical of those that prospered in the city's dynamic industrial economy.

Iron and steel remained dominant. In 1870, 1,375 of Cuyahoga County's 10,063 laborers worked in plants producing iron or iron products. A decade later, 5,821 laborers worked in 38 iron and steel plants, accounting for 29 percent of the city's total manufactured product value. But the Cleveland Business Directory in the 1874 *Atlas of Cuyahoga County, Ohio* suggests the city's economic diversity: There were 18 brewers, 6 bakers and confectioners, 9 carriage and wagon makers, 21 coal dealers, and 4 flouring mills. Also listed were pharmaceutical firms, marble works, oil manufacturers and dealers, and saw and planing mills. During the 1870s, sewing machines, paint and varnish, woolen goods, and ready-to-wear suits and cloaks also became significant parts of the city's industrial base.

Lured by the promise of work in the city's expanding industries, immigrants began to flock to Cleveland following the Civil War. In 1870, 42 percent of the city's 92,829 residents were foreign-born. The largest number of foreign-born had come from Germany (15,855), followed by Ireland (9,964), England (4,530), and Bohemia (786), with lesser totals from other nations. By 1890, the percentage of foreign-born had declined slightly, to 37 percent of Cleveland's population of 261,353. But the dramatic impact of immigration is evident from the fact that fully three-quarters of the city's population was now either foreign-born or the children of foreign-born parents.

Whereas the earliest immigrants to Cleveland had come from Germany and Ireland, those arriving after 1870 also included large numbers of Southern and Eastern Europeans: Poles, Russian Jews, Hungarians, Czechs, Slovaks, Slovenes, Croats, Serbs, Italians, Greeks, and others. While some immigrants sought relief from economic discrimination and religious persecution, the majority of new arrivals came as workers, not as settlers. They were part of a massive and complex migration of labor to the United States and Canada, and, simultaneously, to the industrializing countries of Western Europe. Not every immigrant left Europe with the intention of remaining in America. Many temporary workers, so-called birds of passage, took their earnings and went home. Recent scholarship has shown that a third of American immigrants returned to their countries of origin in the years from 1899 to 1924. In addition to the availability of work, reasons for coming to Cleveland included friends and relatives already settled here and the city's location on the national arteries of communication—the railroads. By 1872, the influx of immigrants was so great that the city posted special "emigrant police" at the railroad station to assist new arrivals and protect them from swindlers. The new arrivals came largely from agricultural societies; the vast majority were semiskilled and unskilled laborers who readily filled the city's need for an expanded labor force.

Czechs, the first of the Slavic nationalities to immigrate to America, came to Cleveland as early as 1850. They initially settled in the vicinity of Croton Street, a rural district south of Woodland Avenue. With the growth of the city, they moved steadily south and east, settling on subdivided farms along the south side of Kingsbury Run. Many found work in the Newburgh mills of the Cleveland Rolling Mill Company or in the refineries of Standard Oil. By 1880, there were 5,433 Czechs in the city; by 1890, there were 10,287. Cleveland became one of the largest Czech cities in the world, ranking fourth, after Prague, Vienna, and Chicago. Unlike most immigrant groups, the Czechs worked largely at skilled trades—as masons, carpenters, tailors, shoemakers, coopers, bakers, and brewers.

Cleveland's Yugoslavs—Slovenes, Croats, and Serbs—began arriving in significant numbers in the 1890s. They established homes near the plants where they worked, especially near the industrial district along St. Clair Avenue and in Collinwood near the shops of the Lake Shore & Michigan Southern Railroad. Slovaks, who arrived in Cleve-

Hiram House, a social settlement founded in 1896, helped promote the Americanization of immigrants as depicted by this "melting pot" float it sponsored in the 1919 Community Fund parade. The Western Reserve Historical Society.

land beginning in the 1870s, initially settled south of Public Square in the Haymarket district, then relocated along Buckeye Road in what then were the outskirts of the city. Others settled on the near West Side, in Tremont, and at Woodland Hills Avenue (East 93rd Street) and Aetna Road. All these areas of settlement were near manufacturing plants, Slovak men furnishing the fundamental heavy labor for many of the city's largest industries, while many of the young women worked in the city's cigar and candy factories.

A number of ethnic entrepreneurs rose to prominence and provided their countrymen with employment. Among them was Theodor Kundtz, a cabinetmaker from Hungary who immigrated to Cleveland in 1873 and established his own company to supply cabinets to the White Sewing Machine Company. Kundtz built an extensive plant at Winslow and Center streets in the Flats. By 1900, he employed 2,500 skilled craftsmen, many of them fellow countrymen living on the near West Side within walking distance of the plant.

Another important success story was that of Frank J. Vlchek, a young Czech immigrant. Fired by letters from his two sisters in Cleveland, Vlchek arrived in the city on 25 March 1889, at age 18. Vlchek was trained as a blacksmith, and he worked at that trade for several years before opening his own shop on Central Avenue. Later, he established a tool factory on Quincy Avenue. By 1918, the Vlchek Tool Company employed about four hundred workers (mostly Czechs) and ranked among the nation's largest automobile-tool manufacturers. Vlchek was also a writer, and in his autobiography, *Povídka Mého Života* (*The Story of My Life*), published in 1928, he recalled his first impressions of Cleveland and his initial struggles as a stranger in a new land—experiences that must have been shared by many of the city's immigrants.

Upon arriving in Cleveland, Vlchek traveled by horsecar to Garden (Central) and Brooker (East 76th) streets, a new Czech neighborhood where his sister Rezinka lived. After a night's sleep, he awoke to familiar sounds:

> That it was a Czech settlement I ascertained as soon as I came out of the house: I heard Czech being spoken on every side. Even a street merchant, whose jaded mare was dragging a wagon through the muddy street, cried his wares in Czech: "Banany, oranže, mrkev, jablky!" ["Bananas, oranges, carrots, apples!"] I was amazed that this man dared to shout in Czech in this fashion, when he was in a foreign country. . . . The house in which my brother-in-law Frantisek and sister Rezinka lived stood behind two other houses, and the three together were called Lisy's Village, and it truly did look just like a Czech village. In the space before the houses, children, chickens, ducks, dogs and cats ran about, and there was not a blade of grass to be seen.

Vlchek was astonished that "a Czech like our landlord Lisy could become the owner of several houses in America," whereas "an opportunity to become rich so quickly does not arise in Bohemia even for the most industrious and thrifty of people."

Vlchek described his search for work and a disheartening first look at the Cuyahoga River. In the company Krejčiček, a fellow Czech who offered to serve as his spokesman, Vlchek stopped first, without success, at the Standard Oil works:

We walked along Broadway and when we came to the older quarter [we] branched off around the Rockefeller barrel works and oil plants; we took our stand before a gate where about twenty people were already waiting. They all looked longingly toward the closed gates, wondering when they would open and allow them to pour through. At last the gates were opened. We all went in; a clerk came, chose about four men and waved the rest of us away. Everything in the vicinity reeked of oil so that it was difficult to breathe. We walked farther along the valley, and crossed a wooden bridge over a river whose like I had never seen in all my life: yellowish black rings of oil circled on its surface, like grease on soup; the water was yellowish, thick, full of clay, stinking of oil and sewage. The water heaped rotting wood on both banks of the river; everything was dirty and neglected. I didn't try to hide from my friend the fact that I was disappointed by this view of an American river. How beautiful the sight of the clear river at home!—winding along through colorful meadows, between alders and willows whose roots made the banks secure! Krejčiček gave me some advice: "My boy, you must forget Bohemia; you're in America now."

Isolated in ethnic enclaves—Warszawa, Dutch Hill, the Angle, Kouba, Birdtown, and Haymarket were among the colorful names of Cleveland's immigrant neighborhoods at the turn of the century—the foreign-born were often feared, distrusted, and resented by their native hosts. Immigrants commonly developed their own social institutions, seeking solace and company in foreign-language churches, national halls, social clubs, and voluntary associations devoted to sports or the fine arts. The cafe and the boardinghouse were other important hubs. The neighborhood provided a sense of community and cohesiveness, while the nationality newspaper was an important source of news and information.

Cleveland's blacks, meanwhile, tripled in number between 1880 and 1900, but their proportion remained fairly constant—slightly over 1 percent of the city's population. At the close of Reconstruction (1877), there were just over two thousand blacks in Cleveland. Most resided on the East Side, although before the 1880s no ward was more than 5 percent black, and no segregated neighborhoods existed. Integrated facilities were the rule in most of the city's restaurants, lecture halls, and other public facilities. Discrimination existed, to be sure— the Academy of Music barred black patrons from its dress circle, for example—but was not, at least before 1890, typical of conditions in Cleveland. Economic opportunities for nineteenth-century blacks appear to have been more abundant than they would be after 1900; in 1870, one-third of the black male work force was employed in skilled trades, and nearly 30 percent of the heads of households owned property. The spirit of racial fairness was perhaps most evident in the city's schools, which had been integrated since the 1840s; in 1871, an editorial in the *Cleveland Leader* (13 January) asserted that there was "no sound or reasonable objection" to integration of the schools and that "opposition to it springs wholly from that small and narrow prejudice which is no longer tolerable in this country."

The late nineteenth century was marked by unprecedented labor unrest. Cleveland employed 56,919 in 1880. Ten thousand—almost 18 percent—were women and girls working as domestic servants, laundresses, seamstresses, teachers, and clerks. Generally, wages in the city's larger industries tended to be the same as, or slightly less than, the average paid elsewhere in the United States, according to the *Tenth Census* (1880). The 10-hour day was the common minimum, but in 1886 street railway employees worked a 16- to 18-hour day with two minutes for meals. American labor became increasingly conscious of the inequities of unrestricted capitalism and turned to collective action. Strikes became an almost monthly occurrence after 1867, and conditions became even more acute following the Panic of 1873, which precipitated widespread wage cuts and unemployment.

Throughout the United States, 1877 was a year of recession and labor unrest. In July, in response to wage cuts and work-rule grievances, railroad workers nationwide began one of the most violent strikes in American history. In Cleveland, workers at the Collinwood Yards of the Lake Shore & Michigan Southern struck at noon on 23 July, and those on other Cleveland lines soon followed. Mayor William Grey Rose called up local militia to preserve order. Cleveland experienced a work stoppage, including a halt to freight service, but strikers remained peaceful. Such was not the case at Standard Oil, where the coopers union staged a violent but abortive strike. There, wages had declined since 1872. In 1877, further cuts were announced, reducing wages to an average of fifty-six cents a day. Strike leaders, among them Czech socialists Frank Skarda and Leopold J. Palda, called for a city-wide walkout of all workers earning less than a dollar a day. The coopers were joined by bricklayers, cigarmakers, and others, but the strike disintegrated after strikers' wives attacked police, igniting a riot. A strike at Cleveland Rolling Mill the same year also met with failure.

The labor issue exemplified the "intellectual barrier" that separated old and new attitudes about the rights and obligations of employer and employee. The conflicting attitudes resulted in strikes, struggles over union organization, and theoretical discussions in newspapers and from rostrums, soapboxes, and pulpits. Although many Clevelanders admitted that labor had cause for complaint, few were prepared to admit that something should, or could, be done about it. The clergy, by and large, sided with capitalism and advised laborers to accept an unfortunate situation. Meanwhile, the labor unrest frightened and outraged conservative Clevelanders. In a letter to his father-in-law Amasa Stone on 24 July 1877, the diplomat John Hay expressed alarm over the "rebellion of foreign workmen." "The town is full of thieves and tramps waiting and hoping for a riot," he wrote. When construction began on an armory complete with loopholes in 1879, not a few Clevelanders viewed it as a means of protection from agitators.

Labor warfare temporarily subsided following the collapse of the strikes of 1877 but was soon rekindled. During the spring and summer of 1882, the Cleveland Rolling Mill Company resisted attempts at unionization by importing Polish and Czech workers to replace strikers and by calling on municipal police to preserve order. Public opinion, molded by the newspapers, supported the "right to work." In spite of a resounding defeat, Cleveland labor continued to agitate over wages, hours, and union recognition. In 1885, a more massive and violent strike occurred. When Cleveland Rolling Mill president William Chisholm announced a wage cut, twenty-five hundred workers walked out. Imported Poles and Czechs proved not to have been a permanent solution to the company's labor problems, for, as the *Cleveland Press* (6 July 1885) wryly noted at the height of the trouble, "striking Poles and Bohemians are using the very revolvers given them three years

ago to 'protect' themselves . . . to intimidate their employers now."
Chisholm countered with a lockout on 1 August 1885, but eventually
was forced to capitulate and restore the previous wage scale. Workers
returned to their jobs, but the expected unionization did not occur.

By 1890, little had been accomplished to eliminate the roots of the
conflict, but the battle lines were drawn more sharply and public support for labor had grown. The Federation of Organized Trades and
Labor Unions (later the American Federation of Labor), organized in
Cleveland in 1882, gave rise to increased agitation for improved working conditions and shorter hours, and by 1900 there were a hundred
unions in the city. The final serious conflict of the period was a strike
by the Amalgamated Association of Street Car Men during the summer of 1899. Streetcar boss Henry A. Everett hired men from Buffalo
and St. Louis to take the place of striking Clevelanders. This action
incited ten days of rioting, as strikers and sympathizers stoned cars
and the non-union operators. Cars were burned, wires cut, switches
blown up, barriers placed in the paths of cars. A passenger boycott
proved successful, but the established order maintained a solid front
against labor. *Cleveland Town Topics* (2 September 1899) called for
blood—"The answer for every stone should be a bullet; not fired into
the air, but at the rioter"—and union resistance dwindled. But labor
had won support and sympathy from the general public, and the century ended on a note of embittered determination on both sides.

Cleveland's rapid urbanization brought with it new and complicated
social problems. Charitable organizations had proliferated following
the Civil War, and by 1880 dozens of orphanages, homes for the aged,
and soup houses were operating, usually under the aegis of religious
denominations. Individual and church-sponsored welfare work, which
had been relatively satisfactory before the 1870s, proved sorely inadequate in a rapidly growing and increasingly anonymous city. There
were new, enlarged demands for relief, and caring for the poor became
a permanent part of urban, industrial life in Cleveland.

The complications of industrialization made old systems of charity
ineffective—financial depressions, for one thing, were far more
serious—and leadership gradually shifted from religious sponsorship

352   FRANK LESLIE'S ILLUSTRATED NEWSPAPER.   [JULY 18, 1885.

Frank Leslie's Illustrated Newspaper *depicted the violence which took place during the Cleveland Rolling Mill Strike of 1885.* The Western Reserve Historical Society.

to large, secular organizations designed to perform charity more effi-
ciently. In 1881, the Charity Organization Society (known as Bethel
Associated Charities after it joined with the Bethel Union in 1884)
was formed to coordinate fundraising. Its mission was to reduce va-
grancy and idleness, eliminate "injudicious giving," protect the community from "imposters," make work the basis of relief, and serve only
"deserving" cases. This initial effort to organize charity, however, was
dwarfed by the increasing severity of late-nineteenth-century problems.

The Panic of 1893 caused widespread unemployment and suffering.
"This city is fairly overrun with idle men . . . begging for work and
food from door to door," commented *The Citizen*, a socialist newspaper
edited by printer Max S. Hayes, on 8 July that year. Estimates of
Cleveland's unemployed ranged from eight thousand to twenty thousand. Bethel provided soup and temporary work chopping wood, but
the acute nature of the situation underscored the inadequacy of Cleveland's relief agencies. On May Day (1 May), 1894, riots broke out
among the unemployed, who condemned city leaders for their ineffective relief measures. The following year, Hayes bluntly criticized the
Charity Ball hosted by a well-meaning elite: "Why don't these people
who are so ready to make an excuse of poverty to dance and make
merry consume half the time they waste . . . to enquire as to the
cause of poverty?" (*The Citizen*, 13 April 1895).

Partly in reaction to the new social gospel, which stressed poverty's
root in economic and social inequality, charitable organizations outside
the Bethel umbrella continued to multiply, caring for orphans, alcohol-
ics, unwed mothers, and the elderly. During this period, women actively participated in a variety of charitable endeavors and social reform movements. The Woman's Christian Temperance League (later
the Woman's Christian Temperance Union), founded in Cleveland in
1874, championed the legal prohibition of alcohol in the belief that
drunkenness was a major cause of poverty and the breakup of the
home. The league targeted the city's saloons, visiting and praying with
saloonkeepers and patrons.

The settlement-house movement in Cleveland had its beginnings in
the 1890s as an attempt by the middle class, especially women, to alle-

Established in 1901, the Visiting Nurse Association provided assistance to the needy in Cleveland's immigrant neighborhoods, often assisting, as shown in this 1920 view, in the care of infants and children. The Cleveland Press Collection, Cleveland State University.

viate the dislocation caused by massive immigration and unrestricted economic growth. In the Haymarket district, a crowded immigrant "port of entry" southwest of Public Square, the Friendly Inn Social Settlement arose out of the temperance union's Central Friendly Inn, established in 1874. In 1896, George A. Bellamy established Hiram House on Orange Avenue to serve poor immigrants living in the city's Central-Woodland neighborhood. Goodrich House (later renamed Goodrich-Gannett after longtime director Alice Gannett), initially located at St. Clair Avenue and Bond (East 6th) Street, was founded the following year to supplement the parish work of the Old Stone Church. Both Hiram and Goodrich settlements were materially aided by the philanthropist Flora Stone Mather. Farther east, Alta House was established to serve the Italian community that had grown up on

Murray Hill. Aided by a substantial gift from John D. Rockefeller (and named for his daughter), Alta House hired a visiting nurse and maintained a medical dispensary, public baths, a laundry, and a playground. Almost a dozen such settlements were operating in Cleveland by the 1920s, offering social, recreational, and educational programs for the poor.

The rapidly growing city faced increasingly complex problems of municipal management. Each decade was marked by a virtual doubling of the population, overburdening city services and challenging Cleveland to keep up with the demand. Until the early 1890s, Cleveland continued to operate under the municipal charter issued in 1852. Under it, the mayor was little more than a figurehead, and the city approached each new problem by creating a special board or commission, either elected or appointed, to deal with it—police, fire, health, parks, waterworks, and others. There was little accountability to the public, and lucrative contracts were commonly steered to political favorites. By the late 1880s, municipal affairs were so intolerable that leading citizens demanded a more efficient form of government.

In 1891, the city adopted the Federal Plan (named for its resemblance to the national government structure), establishing the mayor as the executive head of city government with the authority to appoint directors of six departments—public works, police, fire, accounts, law, and charities and correction. The notion that "good government" would now be restored was quickly dispelled with the election of Robert E. McKisson in 1895. McKisson's old-style machine politics and abuse of power sparked creation of the nonpartisan Municipal Association (later the Citizens League) in 1896. The good-government group, led by Harry A. Garfield, son of the late President James A. Garfield, included such leading industrialists as Samuel Mather, David Z. Norton, and John Sherwin. The Municipal Association helped oust McKisson in 1899 and later promoted the city's experiment with the city manager form of government.

Cleveland made gradual improvements to its infrastructure during this period. By 1890, 69 of the city's 462 miles of streets were paved. Travel between the East and West sides was improved with the opening of the Superior Avenue Viaduct in 1878 and the Central Avenue Viaduct a decade later. Cleveland remained acutely aware of the importance of its harbor and port facilities, and their improvement became a perpetual preoccupation of the city's Board of Trade. Beginning in 1877, Congressional appropriations provided for construction and maintenance of a harbor of refuge protected by breakwalls, allowing docks and piers to be built along the lakefront in addition to those on the river.

The electric streetcar made its debut in Cleveland on 26 July 1884, and, following a brief experiment with cable cars in the late 1880s, all but two lines in Cleveland were electrified by 1894. In 1893, competing electric lines were unified into two companies: the Cleveland City Railway Company (embracing the Superior, St. Clair, Woodland, and West Side lines) and the Cleveland Electric Railway Company (embracing the Broadway, Newburgh, East Cleveland, and South Side lines). These were known, respectively, as the "Little Consolidated" and the "Big Consolidated." With the opening of Ohio's first intercity traction line in 1895, connecting Cleveland and Akron, Public Square became the hub of an extensive network of lines. Within a decade, half a dozen electric "interurbans," as they were called, carried passengers and freight between the cities of northern Ohio, providing cheap and efficient transportation and further opening outlying areas to development.

Chicago's Columbian Exposition in 1893 prompted national awareness of the need for city planning and the development of public parks. In Cleveland, the groundwork was laid for the city's Group Plan of public buildings, and by 1896 some 1,200 acres of parkland (much of it donated by leading citizens) had been acquired and improved. Following a plan prepared by Boston landscape architect Ernest Bowditch, the city's parks took the form of romantically landscaped "pleasure grounds," with winding carriage drives and picturesque lakes. Although beautiful, the parks were located too far away from the Clevelanders who most needed them. The city's water supply, meanwhile, was extended with the opening in 1885 of the Fairmount and Kinsman reservoirs, and in 1896 construction began on a new water intake tunnel, 9 feet in diameter and 4 miles offshore, out of the path of sewage discharge; it was finally completed in 1904, following an appalling number of casualties. The successful management of other city services proved more elusive. The city's waste water continued to be discharged untreated into the Cuyahoga River and its tributaries. In 1880, Mayor Rensselaer R. Herrick termed these waterways "open sewers" and warned that something must be done, but in 1897 the city still discharged 50 million gallons of untreated sewage into Lake Erie each day. Industry, meanwhile, shrouded the city in smoke and abatement efforts proved futile.

Public and private schools expanded rapidly in the late nineteenth century. Wood-frame "relief schools" were commonly erected for the temporary housing of a rapidly fluctuating public school population.

Cleveland's public schools enrolled more than 100,000 students at various levels when this photograph of a typical classroom was taken in 1917. The Cleveland Press Collection, Cleveland State University.

Although charges of overcrowding, unsanitary conditions, and political manipulation appeared periodically in the newspapers, some new school buildings—especially the Gothic-style Central High School, erected in 1878—were the pride of the community. Beginning in 1884, manual training was offered after school. By this date, there were 123 parochial schools in the city, and private, independent schools—among them, University School (1890), Laurel School (1896), and Hathaway Brown (1886)—gradually were established to offer a less crowded and more individualized program for children of the elite. Higher education also made important strides. Leonard Case, Jr., founded the Case School in 1880 to provide advanced technical education. The Cleveland Medical College, a branch of Western Reserve College in Hudson, Ohio, had been established in Cleveland in 1845; in 1882, the parent college moved to Cleveland, lured by a gift of $500,000 and 43 acres of land from Amasa Stone. The same decade saw the opening of the Cleveland School of Art (1882, later the Cleveland Institute of Art), the Cleveland School of Music (1884), and St. Ignatius College (1886, later John Carroll University).

The late nineteenth century witnessed the speculative construction of row upon row of mostly wooden houses. These commonly took the form of detached "workers' cottages," modest one-and-one-half- or two-story houses, with their gabled ends facing the street. To maximize profits, two houses were often built on a single city lot, one behind the other. The dispersal of industry over a relatively wide area probably forestalled the erection of tenements in Cleveland. The number of inhabitants per dwelling increased slightly during the last quarter of the nineteenth century, but the average in 1890 of 5.96 persons per dwelling was well below that of many other American industrial cities.

The most affluent Clevelanders still lived on Euclid Avenue, but Glenville and the Clifton Park section of Lakewood had begun to attract wealthy Clevelanders. In 1895, University Circle was laid out to improve access to the Heights, where real-estate promoters Patrick Calhoun and John Harkness Brown envisioned an exclusive suburban village. Downtown, too, saw an unprecedented building boom: The Arcade (1890) and the Society for Savings (1890), Western Reserve

In 1895, the Euclid-Superior Arcade (opened in 1890) provided an elegant setting for the National Republican League's banquet. The Cleveland Public Library.

(1891), Cuyahoga (1893), Garfield (1893), and New England (1896) buildings—the city's first tall buildings—all opened, as did the architecturally resplendent Sheriff Street Market (1891). After a slow start, the market became a popular trading place for Clevelanders, who, lacking refrigeration, shopped for fresh food daily.

A large population, living in cramped neighborhoods and having some disposable income and access to rail lines, widened the possibilities for entertainment and recreation. Theaters, especially the Euclid

*In 1896, Public Square was the location of a monumental arch tem-
porarily erected as part of Cleveland's Centennial Celebration.* The
Western Reserve Historical Society.

Avenue Opera House on Sheriff Street (built in 1872 and rebuilt in
1893 following a fire), played to large houses. Summer opera could be
heard at Haltnorth's Gardens, a popular German beer garden at
Willson (East 55th) Street and Woodland Avenue. Amusement parks,
including Euclid Beach (1895) and Puritas Springs (1898), made their
debut. League Park—"fit for kings and fans," one newspaper hailed
it—opened on 1 May 1891 at the corner of Dunham (East 66th) and
Lexington, with the legendary Cy Young pitching for the Cleveland
Spiders. Hemmed in by the prosperous middle-class homes of the city's
Hough section, League Park served full-time as the home of Cleveland's major-league baseball team until 1937. In 1890, there were
1,300 saloons in Cleveland. Restaurants had multiplied, and hotels

like the American House, Forest City House—and, especially, the Hollenden House, opened in 1885—were centers of elite male society, which gathered at massive mahogany bars to discuss politics and conduct business.

In the summer of 1896, Cleveland celebrated its centennial with elaborate ceremony. Chimes rang out from Trinity Cathedral, and the Early Settlers Association erected a log cabin on Public Square. One hundred guns fired at midnight by the Ohio Light Artillery marked the close of the city's first century and announced Founder's Day, July 22. Cleveland concluded its first century as one of the nation's most promising industrial and commercial centers. But there were stark reminders that, for some, the city was bleak and inhospitable.

In a compassionate message to Cleveland women of 1996, the Women's Department of the Cleveland Centennial Commission acknowledged that all was not right with their city. The message, enclosed in a time capsule deposited with the historical society, read in part: "We bequeath to you a city of a century, prosperous and beautiful, and yet far from our ideal. Some of our streets are not well lighted; some are unpaved; many are unclean. Many of our people are poor, and some are vainly seeking work at living wages. . . . Some of our children are robbed of their childhood. Vice parades our streets and disease lurks in many places. . . . " In the coming years, Cleveland would go to work to alleviate, if not solve, many of these problems.

CHAPTER EIGHT

The Progressive Years

1900–1914

T he Cleveland of 1900 was four times the size of the city of 1870. Radiating in a broad fan from the lakeshore, Cleveland was a boom town energized by its rapidly expanding population and industries. A time-lapse photograph of the period would have captured the creation of new ethnic settlements and the crowding of old ones; the exodus of Cleveland's native aristocracy from the central city; the rise of remarkable buildings and the proliferation of iron furnaces and ore docks at the water's edge; and the beginnings of the famous Group Plan. Under the leadership of Mayor Tom L. Johnson, the city contributed as never before to the health and happiness of its citizens and received national attention as a center of progressive reform. Journalist Lincoln Steffens judged Cleveland "the best governed city" in the nation.

Between 1900 and 1910, the city's population almost doubled, from 381,768 to 560,663; Cleveland moved up a notch in rank and proudly wore the title of "Sixth City." The astonishing increase represented both territorial growth—Glenville and South Brooklyn were annexed in 1905, Collinwood in 1910—and the continuing influx of foreign immigrants and rural migrants looking for work. One-third of Clevelanders were foreign-born; many only recently had arrived from

Poland, Italy, or Bohemia. They worked in factories, making garments or automobiles, steel or paint. At night, they walked or took the street-car to a modest frame house or to a brick flat with its builder's name— or some other, more exotic designation—inscribed above the door. The Cleveland Industrial Exposition of 1909 showed off the city as one of the outstanding manufacturing centers in the world. According to the 1909 census of manufactures, the Cleveland metropolitan district had 2,230 manufacturing establishments giving employment to 103,709 persons and ranked seventh in the value of its products. The principal industry was iron and steel, closely followed by foundries and machine shops. Automobiles and automobile parts placed third. Other leading industries included slaughtering and meatpacking, men's and women's clothing, printing and publishing, and paint and varnish.

These were heady years for the building industry. The first seven months of 1905 showed a construction total in excess of $5 million, according to *The Ohio Architect and Builder* (August 1905), more than was spent in any year before 1901. The speculative developer flour-ished, platting subdivisions and building identical or nearly identical houses to be sold on mortgage. These were nearly always of wood, two-and-a-half stories tall, with gable end to the street and a front porch; a bay window, classical columns, or "Queen Anne" trim might be added for variety. These years also saw the large-scale construction of apartment buildings and multisuite brick "terraces" (six- to eight-room houses grouped in rows); both were attractive to investors seek-ing a quick return on a relatively small amount of capital.

Commercial activity was concentrated downtown and in the neigh-borhoods during this period. Downtown, numerous fine office build-ings were erected, including the Caxton (1900), Rose (1900), Williamson (1900), Schofield (1902), Citizens (1903), Rockefeller (1905), and Cleveland Athletic Club (1911) buildings. New shops and department stores were established or enlarged, including the May Company (1899), the ten-story Bailey Company store (1903), and the new Sterling & Welch Company (1909) and Halle Brothers Company (1910) stores. In the city's neighborhoods, stores and other services concentrated along the streetcar lines. There, multistory business blocks of brick and stone were built, usually with apartments or offices on the upper floors. Lorain Avenue, Pearl (West 25th) Street, Clark-Fulton, Broadway, St. Clair, Five Points, Buckeye Road, Doan's Corners, and other neighborhood commercial centers all took shape during these years, defining most city neighborhoods as self-contained (and unplanned) collections of homes, schools, factories, stores, and churches.

By 1898, the city's street railways extended as far as the hamlets of Rocky River and Rockport (Kamm's Corners) and South Brooklyn Village (Pearl Street and State Road) on the West Side; and to Euclid Beach Park, Five Points (Collinwood), the Euclid and Mayfield Heights subdivisions (later part of Cleveland Heights), and Warrensville Township on the East Side. As transit facilities improved, residential development spread farther and farther from Public Square. New, speculative allotments enticed those who could afford to move, while landlords in the city's core commonly subdivided single-family houses to accommodate two or more families to meet the insatiable demand of new immigrants for cheap housing.

A 1904 Cleveland Chamber of Commerce report, *Housing Conditions in Cleveland*, stated that despite the widespread public perception that there were no slums in Cleveland, there was indeed "a serious housing problem" in the city and confirmed its cause: "The house built for the single family has now, in many districts, been transformed into a dwelling for several families." Real-estate advertisements of the period illustrate the trend. Large, attractive ads for houses in new allotments cited the advantages of clean air and proximity to streetcar terminals. One lured prospective buyers this way: "Into the Pure Air . . . Is the intention we hear expressed on all sides from those who have lived for years amid the SMOKE AND GRIME of closely built city streets." In contrast were the small, private ads of Clevelanders leaving the city: "FOR SALE—10-room house arranged for 2 families" (*Cleveland Plain Dealer*, 2 April 1910). Thus, gradually but inexorably, the industrial city of the twentieth century was stratified by economic class: the least desirable residences were now in the center city, while the most desirable were in new sections only a streetcar ride away. The most affluent Clevelanders retreated along the lakeshore and into the Appalachian foothills, building brick and stone mansions in Clifton Park (Lakewood), Bratenahl, and Ambler Heights (Cleveland Heights).

Immigration swelled during these years. In reaction to pogroms and harsh economic discrimination, large numbers of Eastern European Jews immigrated to Cleveland. In 1880, there were 3,500 Jews in Cleveland; by 1920, there were 75,000, representing 9 percent of the city's population. They were thickly clustered in the vicinity of Woodland Avenue and Willson (East 55th) Street, where they sought jobs as tailors, carpenters, and grocers. Often economic life in America began with a pushcart, from which the immigrant hawked vegetables on city streets.

Large numbers of Italians, Poles, and Hungarians also arrived during this period. The city's Italian-born population rose from just over 3,000 in 1900 to nearly 11,000 in 1910 and nearly 19,000 in 1920. The first Italians in Cleveland had settled in the lower Central-Woodland district, many working in the produce markets in an area that came to be known as Big Italy. During this period, many settled in Collinwood or in the Little Italy neighborhood at Murray Hill and Mayfield roads; they worked in the embroidery and garment trades, as gardeners, or as stonecutters. Poles had begun arriving in Cleveland by 1870, but the largest influx occurred between 1900 and 1914. By 1920, there were 35,000 Poles in Cleveland, many of whom had settled along Fleet Avenue (at East 65th Street) and worked in the nearby steel mills; this, the largest Polish colony in Cleveland, came to be called Warszawa. Buckeye Road, meanwhile, became the largest of the city's Hungarian settlements during these years. John Weizer, proprietor of a small grocery on Woodland Avenue, sold two thousand lots to his countrymen, and by 1920 the Hungarian community had expanded east along Buckeye to Shaker Square. Modest two-family houses, with double porches and identical floor plans, enabled the investor to become both a homeowner and a landlord.

Many of the city's immigrants were from the peasant villages and small towns of Europe and faced a difficult adjustment to life in American industrial society. Many Clevelanders viewed them with distrust, recoiling at their strange customs and condemning their tendency to settle in groups. The task of assimilation fell largely to the public

*This 1920s backyard scene in Cleveland's "Big Italy" neighborhood
on lower Woodland Avenue suggests some of the housing conditions
confronted by new arrivals to the city.* The Western Reserve Historical Society.

schools, which offered classes in English, citizenship, and housekeep-
ing, and pioneered the creation of medical departments in the schools.
During World War I, the Cleveland Americanization Committee published histories of the city's nationality groups to help improve cross-
cultural understanding and promoted adult classes in English and
citizenship in schools, libraries, social settlements, churches, and
factories. Many Cleveland employers—including Joseph & Feiss,
Ferry Cap & Screw, and Federal Knitting Mills—testified that it was
in their own interest to offer English classes in order to improve labor-
management relations and communication among workers. The city's
branch libraries also aided the foreign-born. Eleanor E. Ledbetter, li-

brarian of the Broadway branch of the Cleveland Public Library for nearly thirty years, had a special sympathy for the city's immigrant groups. The branch offered books in fourteen different languages, developed large Czech and Polish collections, and sponsored nationality programs. To criticism that foreign-language books would discourage the learning of English, Ledbetter replied, "To find books in one's own language is next to finding living friends, and only the exile can appreciate what it means."

Cleveland's black community, meanwhile, was a quiet but growing presence, having increased from 1,300 in 1870, to 3,000 in 1890, to 8,500 in 1910. Migration from other states, especially from the

The Cleveland Public Library's Broadway branch served the city's largest Czech community. Here, area children crowd the branch's reading room. The Cleveland Public Library.

South—part of the general drift of rural inhabitants to cities before World War I—accounted for most of the growth. In contrast to the large and well-defined postwar ghetto that would arise, blacks prior to 1915 were geographically quite dispersed. Census data for 1910 shows that all but 17 of 155 census tracts on the East Side contained some black residents, and no tract was more than 25 percent black. Even in the growing black neighborhood at Central and Scovill avenues between Perry (East 22nd) and Putnam (East 38th) streets, blacks were still a minority and lived in close proximity to white ethnic immigrants, especially Russian Jews and Italians.

While blacks in nineteenth-century Cleveland had been generally integrated into Cleveland society, by the turn of the century racial discrimination became more conspicuous. Blacks were excluded from some hotels, theaters, and restaurants. At the popular Luna Park resort, blacks could enter only on designated "Jim Crow" days; even then, they were not permitted to use the bathing facilities, which were consistently "out of order" on those days only. After 1915, there would be rising hostility toward Cleveland blacks—a reaction, in part, to their increasing numbers and visibility.

Much of the period 1900–1914 was shaped by Mayor Tom L. Johnson, a tough-minded entrepreneur turned reformer who had come to Cleveland in the late 1870s as a street-railway investor and operator. A two-term congressman and ardent advocate of the single-tax theories of Henry George, Johnson articulated the ideas of this reform-minded age, holding popular tent meetings around the city to communicate directly with citizens. Critics likened the meetings to a "circus menagerie," but their informality helped bring immigrants, women, and the unlettered into the political life of the city for the first time. Johnson championed women's suffrage, municipal ownership of utilities, just taxation, and home rule for Ohio's cities. He used his own experience with the "invisible government" of big business to fight monopolies and corruption, spoilsmen and machine politicians. "The greatest movement in the world today may be characterized as the struggle of the people against Privilege," he later wrote in his autobiography (*My*

Story, 1911). That belief formed the theme of Johnson's four terms as mayor, from 1901 to 1909.

Under Johnson's leadership, the city embarked on a host of progressive projects and reforms. "When he was mayor of Cleveland," one historian later wrote of Johnson, "the people for the first time learned that they really owned the parks." Johnson ordered down all "Keep Off the Grass" signs. Mirroring park reform efforts nationwide, he provided playgrounds in the most crowded districts of the city. He built baseball diamonds and basketball and tennis courts, sponsored Sunday band concerts in the parks and ice skating competitions for children, and built public bathhouses in the poorest neighborhoods. He instituted reforms in the city police force and built a model workhouse and reformatory on farmland outside the city. Johnson relentlessly chal-

Cleveland's noted reform mayor, Tom L. Johnson, inspects the work of a city street repair crew ca. 1907. The Western Reserve Historical Society.

lenged the streetcar monopoly he himself once sought to control. He proposed building a municipal light plant, which was finally realized in 1914 with the opening of the largest municipally owned central station in the country. Rapid population growth and the rising cost of living stimulated interest nationwide in efficient and economical food markets, and in 1901 Johnson appointed a market house commission to plan a new West Side Market, which opened in 1912. The first modern, comprehensive building code, adopted in 1904, was another of Johnson's accomplishments.

Perhaps the most permanent legacy of Johnson's tenure as mayor was the city's Group Plan, or Mall. A formal grouping of the city's major public buildings had been urged since 1895 by the Cleveland Architectural Club, especially by teacher and art collector Charles F. Olney. Johnson appointed a Group Plan Commission, consisting of three architects of national stature and chaired by Chicago's Daniel Burnham, in 1902. A year later, in August 1903, the commission presented its recommendations. The plan proposed the demolition and clearance of a large area of squalor northeast of the Public Square, and the symmetrical grouping of the city's public buildings around a broad mall reaching toward the lake. Most of the elements of the Mall so familiar to Clevelanders today—the classically styled federal and county courthouses, public library, city hall, public auditorium, and school administration building grouped around a rectangular promenade—were established in the visionary Group Plan of 1903.

After four terms, the charismatic Johnson narrowly lost to the weak and colorless Herman C. Baehr in 1909, though City Solicitor Newton D. Baker, Johnson's closest advisor, was returned to office. Johnson's defeat is usually attributed to public weariness of the bitter and protracted "streetcar war," which pitted Johnson and the city against the private Cleveland Electric Railway Company, the Chamber of Commerce, and other business interests in the quest for municipal control and a three-cent fare. The conflict was finally settled in 1909 by the Tayler Grant, a transit plan devised by Federal Judge Robert W. Tayler that consolidated all of the city's streetcar lines into the Cleveland Railway Company and assured "good service at the cost of service"; the plan, which attracted national attention, made the company an agent of the city, established an initial three-cent fare, and limited profits to 6 percent.

Baehr's victory in the 1909 mayoral race was engineered by Republican boss Maurice Maschke, whose skillful use of the city's ethnic and minority groups would maintain a powerful hold on Cleveland politics for the next two decades. The Democrats returned to City Hall two years later, however, with the election of Newton D. Baker, who served two terms, then was called to Washington as secretary of war. During Baker's tenure as mayor, a home rule amendment to the Ohio constitution was finally passed, and voters approved a new city charter in 1913. The new charter was modeled on the former Federal Plan, but the mayor's position was strengthened by total control of the administrative branch.

The Cleveland Chamber of Commerce took an active interest in social reform and efficient municipal management during these years despite the enmity of Mayor Johnson, who distrusted its motives. Cleveland had been the first U.S. city to establish a modern Chamber of Commerce (1893, successor to the Board of Trade), and in the early 1900s the chamber was a powerful organization of some sixteen hundred leading businessmen. Ryerson Ritchie, first secretary of the new chamber, molded its vision to include general civic affairs. Committees on health, transportation, education, harbor facilities, and industry focused on a variety of public policy issues. The chamber was instrumental, for example, in passing a tenement law and in carrying out the Group Plan. It initiated a new, comprehensive system of naming streets and numbering buildings; the city adopted the plan, which substituted numbers for the names of north-south streets, in 1905.

The chamber also worked to reform the haphazard distribution of charitable aid. Rapid growth had brought with it manifold welfare problems, and an array of charitable agencies competed for donations from the same small group of wealthy Clevelanders. In 1900, the Chamber of Commerce formed a Committee on Benevolent Associations to work toward creation of a single, secular organization to serve as a clearinghouse for the collection and distribution of charity dollars. The chamber organized the Federation for Charity and Philanthropy in 1913; federation members could participate as beneficiaries of the centralized fundraising campaign if they agreed to eliminate their own fundraising activities and submit to periodic audits. The success of the experiment led to the formation of the Cleveland Community Fund (later the United Way) in 1919, the first in the nation. A full-time staff, using the scientific management methods of modern business, handled collections and publicity. Coordinated giving transferred the burden of charity from the local rich to the community at large and concentrated the control of charity in the hands of businessmen and professional social workers. Also arising from the city's business community during this period, the Cleveland Foundation was established in 1914 by Cleveland Trust Company president Frederick H. Goff. The foundation, the first community trust in the nation, used donations and bequests to underwrite projects of community benefit. Among its first activities was a series of substantive reports on the city's public schools (1916) and criminal justice system (1921).

Opportunities for women, meanwhile, were few. The Cleveland Suffrage League, which focused on gaining the vote in Ohio, worked diligently but unsuccessfully. One notable agency of reform founded and run by Cleveland women was the Consumers League of Ohio. Organized in 1900, the league's initial purpose was to improve the welfare of workers by urging consumer boycotts of businesses not on the league's "white lists" of companies paying fair wages, employing only adults, and providing good working conditions. Beginning in 1909, the league actively campaigned for better working conditions and a minimum wage. The Consumers League was one of the few forums in which women, who were excluded from political life, could engage in meaningful reform activities. Among its leaders were a number of prominent Cleveland women: Alice Gannett, a settlement-house worker and reformer who headed Cleveland's Goodrich House settlement for thirty years; Belle Sherwin, a noted feminist and director of the Cleveland Welfare Federation from 1900 to 1914; and Marie Remington Wing, one of the first of two women elected to the Cleveland city council in 1923.

In the black community, social worker Jane Edna Hunter worked to provide safe living quarters for young, homeless black women in the city, many of whom had migrated from the South. Hunter, a South

In 1912, Cleveland women joined in an unsuccessful campaign to gain the right to vote for Ohio women. Local women would not be enfranchised until the passage of the 19th Amendment in 1920. The Western Reserve Historical Society.

Carolina sharecropper's daughter trained as a nurse, organized the Phillis Wheatley Association (named after the black poet) in 1911. By 1916, 170 women were being housed, fed, and trained at the association's home at East 40th Street and Central Avenue. Essentially conservative, the association was financed and controlled by white Clevelanders in its early years, and most of its graduates before 1930 became domestic servants. Hunter faced opposition from blacks who objected to the establishment of a segregated institution; some saw a direct correlation between the establishment of Phillis Wheatley and the exclusion of blacks from the Young Women's Christian Association. Nevertheless, Hunter persisted in her goal of establishing a safe haven for black women.

The progressive years had blessed Cleveland with efficient and humane government and a remarkable legacy of civic building. Through the efforts of a broad spectrum of reformers, the city had come to grips with some of the worst problems of industrialization. By 1914, Cleveland had lost its enthusiasm for reform. Tom Johnson had died two years after leaving office; Newton Baker was returned to office as mayor, but by a greatly reduced majority. War in Europe now shifted the city's attention to the fight for democracy—at home and abroad.

CHAPTER NINE

Metropolitan Expansion

1915–1929

War in Europe started a chain reaction of broad consequence: it emptied the city of its young men, put an end to large-scale European immigration, and sparked an industrial boom that signaled the beginning of the great migration of Southern blacks to Cleveland. All this occurred against a backdrop of rapid social and cultural change. Automobiles, new bridges, and the first paved highways stimulated metropolitan expansion. Inner-ring suburbs quickly filled with the prosperous middle class. An ambitious new development on high ground east of the city, called Shaker Village, promised "permanency" and protection from commercial and social "invasion." The fine old homes of Euclid Avenue were abandoned or left to charity. But downtown Cleveland remained the economic heart of the city, and on Public Square the largest building project in the city's history—the massive Terminal Tower complex—slowly took shape. In addition to business, meanwhile, the city's leading families occupied themselves with the cultural arts.

Cleveland continued to enjoy its reputation as one of the nation's most progressive and attractive cities. Construction of the Group Plan was successfully advanced with completion of a new public auditorium (1922), main library (1925), and music hall (1929). Cleveland Munici-

Trains of soldiers departed from Cleveland's lakefront Union Depot during the World War I years of 1917 and 1918. Nearly 41,000 Clevelanders joined the services during the war. The Western Reserve Historical Society.

pal Airport opened in 1925, and the Cleveland Metropolitan Park District, urged since 1905 by park engineer William A. Stinchcomb, was established in 1917 for the purpose of encircling metropolitan Cleveland with a chain of parks and boulevards while preserving the county's most scenic areas from development.

The 1920s had a distinctive rhythm, an air of optimism and modernity. Women had won the right to vote and sported new independence with short hair and short skirts. The city's first radio station went on the air and, despite Prohibition, liquor could be readily found at the city's many private clubs. In the new Playhouse Square district at East 14th Street and Euclid Avenue rose a remarkable string of vaudeville and motion picture theaters: the Stillman, Allen, Ohio, State, Palace, and Lake theaters formed the core of the city's nightlife. The Hanna

Theater, also at Playhouse Square, succeeded the Euclid Avenue Opera House in 1921, presenting popular road shows. At Euclid Avenue and East 105th Street, Keith's 105th, the Circle, the University, the Alhambra, and the Park theaters mixed with the Elysium Ice Palace, Bailey's branch department store, nightclubs, and restaurants to form a vibrant "Uptown" district. Nearby, crowds filled League Park to watch the Cleveland Indians (the baseball team had chosen its new moniker in 1915) win the American League pennant and the World Series in 1920.

Wartime prosperity carried into the succeeding decade. The 1920s were marked by a heady industrial expansion and the continuation of Cleveland's strong position (second only to Detroit) as a center of auto-

Cleveland youngsters try to get a glimpse of the action at a 1920 World Series game being played at League Park. The Indians defeated the Brooklyn Dodgers to win their first world championship. The Western Reserve Historical Society.

mobile manufacture. In 1920, Winton, White, Peerless, Chandler, Stearns, Baker, and Ford all were producing vehicles in the city, while the mammoth Fisher Body Company plant, covering 39 acres, opened on Coit Road in 1921. Industrial supremacy made Cleveland a center of the labor movement. The largest of its labor organizations, the Brotherhood of Locomotive Engineers, had built its own office building in 1910 and in 1924 opened its own cooperative bank in the BLE-built Standard Building. Other strong railroad labor organizations headquartered in Cleveland were the Brotherhood of Railroad Trainmen and the Brotherhood of Locomotive Firemen and Enginemen. There were 150 labor unions in the city; most belonged to the American Federation of Labor and worked for better hours, higher wages, and improved working conditions.

In business, the massive empire assembled by two shy, reclusive bachelor brothers epitomized the era of prosperity and left a deep imprint on the city. Oris Paxton Van Sweringen and Mantis James Van Sweringen had begun buying land in the old Shaker community east of the city in 1905. There, they plotted a model suburban community at the very time that wealthy Clevelanders were looking for new luxury housing outside the city. Shaker Heights represented a model residential suburb, with romantic period houses set on curvilinear streets and protected by deed restrictions and architectural guidelines enforced by the Van Sweringen Company. To control 5 miles of needed right of way for a rapid transit line connecting downtown Cleveland with the new suburb, the Van Sweringens acquired the 513-mile Nickel Plate Railroad. Transit operations to the suburb began in 1920, and the population of Shaker Heights grew tenfold in the space of a decade. The Van Sweringens, meanwhile, had built the elegant Hotel Cleveland on Public Square. In 1918, they formed the Cleveland Union Terminals Company and proposed to build a new railroad station at the southwest corner of the Square. Voters approved the plan in 1919, and in 1923 ground was broken for the largest building project in the city's history. Construction of the Cleveland Union Terminal complex continued throughout the decade, eradicating most of the old Haymarket district in its wake, while the Van Sweringens assem-

Women workers at the Glenn L. Martin Company, on St. Clair Avenue, helped produce the major bombing airplane used by the United States after World War I. The Western Reserve Historical Society.

bled a railroad empire that extended their sphere of influence virtually nationwide.

Cleveland's first families, most of whom now lived beyond the city's borders, endowed important cultural institutions during these years. The Cleveland Orchestra was organized in 1918; a decade later, John L. Severance announced his gift of a concert hall (Severance Hall, completed in 1931) as a memorial to his wife. The Cleveland Museum of Art, housed in a Neoclassic temple framed by the elegantly landscaped grounds of Wade Park, opened in 1916, representing the gifts of several wealthy Clevelanders. Other institutions begun during this period would remain important features of the city's cultural life: the Cleveland Music School Settlement (1912), the Playhouse Settlement (1915, later Karamu House), the Cleveland Play House (1916), the Cleveland Institute of Music (1920), and the Cleveland Museum of Natural History (1920). In *Memoir of a Modernist's Daughter* (1988), Eleanor Munro recalled this bountiful era of cultural philanthropy in Cleveland:

> The settlers put great store on benevolent institutions. They started libraries, academies, clinics, endowed galleries of natural history and fine arts. In the era of robber baron capitalists, the institutions profited. . . . The academy became a university. The clinic acquired marble halls. The picture gallery became a museum rich in bronzes, tapestries, suits of armor, and portraits of kings. When I was a child, descendants of the original founders still lived along the lake in granite mansions hung with El Grecos. Rembrandts and Cezannes. Solemn with responsibility, they promenaded at cultural events, Edwardian men in dinner suits and plain, intelligent women in great-girthed brocaded gowns.

The city's population and neighborhoods were in a state of flux during these years. Suburban growth had been slow before the war; the city, in fact, had continued to expand in territory and population by annexing nearby towns and unincorporated areas. But suburban voters began rejecting bids for annexation to Cleveland (Lakewood in 1922, Parma in 1931), and with the annexation of West Park Village in 1922 and Miles Heights Village in 1932, Cleveland was territorially arrested at 76 square miles. While the city's population continued to increase, growing from 796,841 in 1920 to 900,429 in 1930, some suburban areas were growing at a faster rate. A map of changes in the metropolitan population during this decade shows that outlying areas, including the suburbs of Cleveland Heights, Shaker Heights, Garfield Heights, and Parma, enjoyed the greatest growth (500 percent or more), while the urban core experienced decreases of 10 percent or more. The automobile made this outward migration possible.

Per capita ownership of automobiles soared during these years. In 1916, there were 61,000 automobiles registered in Cuyahoga County; ten years later, there were 211,000. The growing use of motorcars greatly enlarged the range of residential locations within a half-hour's

─────── WHAT ───────

Happiness and Independence

MEANS

TO own your own home
TO have your own garden
TO raise your own fruit and chickens
TO live where the air is clean and your children have every chance to be strong and healthy

YOU can have all this by buying

─────── IN ───────

RANDALL FARMS

¼—½ and ACRE LOTS **$250.00** AND UP

10 per cent Down and 2 per cent a Month

FREE DEED IN CASE OF DEATH

Automobile service to property free of obligation upon application to

Suburban Estates Company

236 Engineers Building.

PHONE MAIN 3828   CENTRAL 3029-L

New housing developments on Cleveland's southeast side were created in the years just before and after World War I. Many, such as these in Garfield Heights, catered to immigrants and the children of immigrants. The Western Reserve Historical Society.

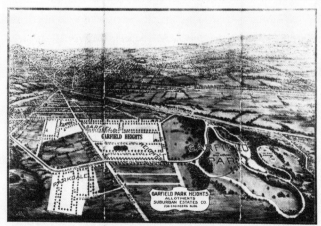

GARFIELD HEIGHTS
WILL HAVE
GRADED STREETS, WATER, SIDEWALKS, SHADE TREES, GAS AND ELECTRICITY

Located on E. 99th, 104th Sts. and Turney Rd. near Garfield Blvd. and adjoining Garfield Park.
The East 105th Street 3c Car Line runs direct to our Allotments, and Transfers to all Car Lines on the East Side

drive of the workplace, completing the transformation of residential patterns begun with electric streetcars and spawning new roadside businesses, including gas stations, auto showrooms, repair shops, and parking lots. Even as the automobile widened the possibilities for housing, travel, and recreation, it widened the economic gap between city and suburb, leaving at the city's core the most recently arrived and least affluent Clevelanders; by 1934, two-thirds of automobiles in the county were owned by middle-class families living in the suburbs.

With its large population of Germans and Eastern Europeans, many of whom were unskilled and unorganized workers living under precarious economic conditions, Cleveland briefly became an important center of the socialist movement during this period. In 1911, the Socialist Party candidate for mayor, Charles E. Ruthenberg, had captured 10 percent of the vote; in 1917, Ruthenberg, who had aligned himself with the Communist Party following the Bolshevik Revolution in Russia, won nearly a third of the 100,000 votes cast in the race. On May Day (1 May), 1919, a parade of socialist sympathizers sparked a nine-hour period of rioting downtown and in scattered parts of the city. Two persons were killed and hundreds were arrested. The riots, together with the bombing of Mayor Harry L. Davis's home the following month (attributed to "radicals"), hardened antiforeign feeling and helped cripple the socialist movement in Cleveland.

The distrust of ward politicians supported by the city's foreign-born was one of the motivating forces behind the demand by good-government advocates, including the Citizens League, for a city manager plan. Following on the heels of several incompetent mayoral administrations, Cleveland became the first large city in the country to experiment with the city manager form of government. The new charter, approved by voters in 1921, abolished the traditional ward system and provided for a professional manager selected by the city council to administer the city's affairs. The city was divided into four districts, from each of which five to seven council members were elected at large. Two able city managers, William R. Hopkins and Daniel E. Morgan, served from 1924 to 1931, when the experiment was discontinued. By then, many of the plan's most ardent supporters had moved to the suburbs, and city residents viewed it as too remote from their needs.

Cleveland's black ghetto had its beginning in this period. The war had effectively ended the period of large-scale European immigration. Following the conflict, restrictive legislation—including the Quota Act of 1921 and the Immigration Restriction Act of 1924—slowed foreign immigration to a trickle. Just as peasants from Eastern Europe had replenished the supply of manual laborers who earlier had come from Germany, Great Britain, and Ireland, Southern blacks were now recruited to fill the need. Labor agents representing Northern industrialists induced blacks to migrate by offering free train tickets and the promise of good jobs. As news of life in the North filtered back, the migration became self-generating. The city's black population rose from 8,448 in 1910 to 34,451 in 1920—a 308 percent increase. "There is no mistaking what is going on," the *Cleveland Advocate*, a black newspaper, editorialized on 28 April 1917, "it is a REGULAR EXODUS."

Blacks fleeing racial intolerance and poverty in the South had been coming north since the Civil War. But there was no precedent for the Great Migration, as it was called, that accompanied the war. The city was suddenly faced with assimilating large numbers of newcomers who, typically, were neither educated nor accustomed to urban life. Migrants, meanwhile, faced a shortage of housing, limited social services, and racial hostility. The housing shortage in the black community reached crisis proportions. Boarding and rooming houses were packed. Single-family houses were divided into "suites." The Cleveland Real Estate Board in 1917 reported the need for an additional 10,000 units to house the newcomers, while the Chamber of Commerce the following year reported that blacks were paying 65 percent more than whites for comparable housing.

Poet Langston Hughes came to live in Cleveland during these years, and in his autobiography, *The Big Sea* (1940), he recalled the difficulties blacks faced:

Newsboys for the Call and Post *newspaper gathered at the paper's office after a 1930s subscription sales contest. Many of their parents had come to Cleveland during the Great Migration of black Americans from the South in the years during and after World War I.* The Western Reserve Historical Society.

I had no sooner graduated from grammar school in Lincoln than we moved from Illinois to Cleveland. My stepfather sent for us. He was working in a steel mill during the war, and making lots of money. But it was hard work, and he never looked the same afterwards. . . . Rents were very high for colored people in Cleveland, and the Negro district was extremely crowded, because of the great migration. It was difficult to find a place to live. We always lived, during my high school years, either in an attic or basement, and paid quite a lot for such inconvenient quarters. White people on the east side of the city were moving out of their frame houses and renting them to Negroes at double and triple the rents they could receive from others. An eight-room house with one bath would be cut up into apartments and five or six families crowded into it, each two-room kitchenette apartment renting for what the whole house had rented for before.

Prior to the war, Cleveland's Central Avenue district housed the largest number of the city's blacks. During the Great Migration, this area absorbed most of the new arrivals, accelerating residential segregation. As blacks moved into the area between Euclid and Woodland avenues, and filled in areas contiguous to existing black neighborhoods along Central and Scovill avenues, Russian and Italian enclaves dispersed to other areas of the city. Unlike these immigrant groups, Cleveland's blacks did not disperse as new migrants arrived from the South; instead, the black community expanded in size even as it was further restricted in area. "The area in which ninety percent of the Negroes live has decreased since 1910," Cleveland statistician Howard Whipple Green reported in 1930, even though, during these two decades, the black community had grown 851 percent (from 8,448 to 71,899). The Woodland-Central neighborhood deteriorated rapidly, suffering higher rates of infant mortality, pneumonia, tuberculosis, and venereal disease than other areas of the city. Central Avenue became a hotbed of gambling, prostitution, and crime; law enforcement was lax in the "Roaring Third," as whites called the area.

The postwar years saw the intensification of racism and discrimination, and blacks increasingly experienced unequal treatment in places of public accommodation. The YMCA restricted blacks to a single branch of Cedar Avenue in the 1920s, while the YWCA continued its policy on excluding blacks altogether. The National Association for the Advancement of Colored People, founded in 1914, was vitalized in the 1920s with new leadership and a larger population base on which to draw. The organization intervened in cases of racial discrimination—for example, when the Higbee Company refused to allow black women to try on articles of clothing. While the growth of the ghetto enabled two new black members, E. J. Gregg and Clayborne George, to join the city council in 1927, the racial inequality and slum conditions that plagued Cleveland's black ghetto were beyond the scope of a few councilmen—and, it would become apparent, even the city—to solve.

Photographs of Cleveland's immigrant ghetto—the lower Woodland-Broadway intersection, long since erased by freeway construction—freeze the historical moment in time. The streets, of stone or brick, are laid with ribbons of rail, and overhead is a maze of trolley wires. Curb markets line the sidewalks amid makeshift storefronts and covered sheds. Horse-drawn carts are still in use; watermelons and crates of live poultry are stacked curbside. A billboard advertises the Ringling Bros. Barnum & Bailey Circus, appearing for two days on the lakefront showgrounds at the foot of Ninth Street. On the door of one decrepit dwelling there is a sign: "Rooms for Rent." On other neglected buildings are signs reading, "We move June 1st to Northern Ohio Food Terminal." In the distance rises the spire of the Terminal Tower, nearing completion. The year is 1929.

The new food terminal, a development of the Van Sweringens'

Cleveland's old Haymarket district near Broadway Avenue and East 9th Street stands in contrast to the almost new Terminal Tower in the early 1930s. The Western Reserve Historical Society.

Nickel Plate Railroad, opened on 3 June, consolidating and modernizing Cleveland's system of wholesale food distribution. Later that year, on 23 October, the first passenger train entered the new Union Terminal on Public Square carrying the Van Sweringens and Erie Railroad officials. No one on that celebratory train could have known that, in just six days, the bubble of prosperity would burst, bringing a psychological if not actual end to Cleveland's dominance as a national industrial and urban power.

CPM

Part Four

TOWARD THE POSTINDUSTRIAL CITY

CHAPTER TEN

An End to Prosperity

1930–1939

"It is something to make anyone glad he is a Clevelander." So was the *Plain Dealer* moved to comment on 19 August 1927, the day after steelworkers unfurled a flag from the topmost peak of the Terminal Tower and doffed their hats with pride. The "city within a city" was nearing completion. Development of the Cleveland Union Terminal group—consisting of the Terminal Tower, with the city's new railroad station below grade; the Builders' Exchange, Medical Arts, and Midland buildings; and the Higbee department store (the Hotel Cleveland had been built in 1918)—was the biggest real-estate news in the city's history. It had a profound impact, eliminating a large area of squalor and making Public Square, the traditional center of business and civic life, once again the focus of downtown. It left Cleveland with the mark of a metropolis on it. In conceiving and building so comprehensive a project, Cleveland's Van Sweringen brothers created not only a profitable commercial center but also a new focus for Cleveland's pride and a distinctive visual symbol for the city—a landmark. Dedication of the new $150-million Cleveland Union Terminal was the outstanding civic event of 1930. On 28 June, some 2,500 of the city's leaders gathered for lunch in the station's main concourse. Surrounding them were more than forty shops and restaurants operated by Harvey, Inc., said to be the world's largest unified merchandising service operated in conjunction with a railroad passenger station. Cleveland's new station handled eighty trains a day, as well as the rapid-transit line serving the Van Sweringens' new residential development of Shaker Heights. *Railway Age* called it "a passenger terminal which ranks in magnitude and completeness with the best in the country."

Cleveland in 1930 had other reasons to celebrate. The 1920s had been a decade of great industrial, economic, and financial growth; of municipal progress and reform; and of advancement in the arts, medicine, education, and city planning and beautification. Large and important commercial buildings had been erected, including the Federal Reserve Bank and the Ohio Bell Telephone, Hanna, and Union Trust buildings. New theaters and motion-picture palaces had opened at Playhouse Square, and drew in their wake new shops and restaurants. Following on the heels of the turbulent Fred Kohler administration, municipal affairs had been guided by the able city manager William R. Hopkins. The Municipal Airport had been established, and construction of the new Cleveland Municipal Stadium was about to begin. The Board of Education Building was nearing completion, and the city's Group Plan was progressing. Both the Cleveland Public Library and the Public Auditorium had opened. The latter, promoted by the Convention Board of the Chamber of Commerce, attracted some of the country's largest gatherings—143,628 delegates would attend 237 conventions there in 1930—and materially aided the city's bid to become a convention capital. Beyond the city's borders, the development of Lakewood, East Cleveland, Cleveland Heights, and Shaker Heights signaled the first flush of metropolitan expansion.

For Cleveland, the year 1930 marked a watershed in the city's fortunes. The preceding decade had been a heady success, a period best symbolized, perhaps, by the ethereal images produced by the young photographer Margaret Bourke-White of a brawny city ruled and shaped by powerful industries and equally powerful industrialists. In the space of a few months, however, tens of thousands of Clevelanders would be out of work, while more than a few of the city's barons—including the Van Sweringens—would face financial ruin. The depression years 1930–1939 thus mark a distinct period in the city's life—an end to prosperity—from which, it might be argued, Cleveland has never fully recovered.

With a population of 900,429, Cleveland in 1930 was the nation's sixth-largest city, after New York, Chicago, Philadelphia, Detroit, and Los Angeles. With a combined city and county population of 1,201,455, it was the third-most-populated metropolitan area, after New York and Chicago. Startling changes had occurred since 1910. The population of Cuyahoga County outside of Cleveland had more than doubled, and now represented 25 percent of the total population of the county.

	Cleveland	Cuyahoga County	City as % of County
1910	560,663	637,425	88%
1920	796,841	943,495	84%
1930	900,429	1,201,455	75%

The four largest adjacent cities—Lakewood, East Cleveland, Cleveland Heights, and Shaker Heights—in 1930 had a combined population of 178,904. These four cities, accounting for slightly more than 4 percent of the county's population in 1910, by 1930 accounted for as much as 15 percent.

For thirty years, statistician Howard Whipple Green studied and reported on population trends in Greater Cleveland. His first major study, *Population Characteristics by Census Tracts, Cleveland, Ohio*, published by the Plain Dealer Publishing Company in 1931, contained a wealth of information about the city's people and revealed trends that could not otherwise be discerned. Cleveland's foreign-born white population had declined, from 30.1 percent of the city's population in 1920 to 25.5 percent in 1930. The greatest number of the city's foreign-born had come from Czechoslovakia (15.1 percent) and Poland (14.2 percent). Other countries with large numbers in Cleveland included Italy (10.3 percent), Germany (9.8 percent), Hungary (8.3 percent), Yugoslavia (8.0 percent), and Russia (6.6 percent). According to Green, each foreign-born, white, non-English-speaking group occupied a distinctly different section of the five-city metropolitan area (Cleveland, Lakewood, East Cleveland, Cleveland Heights, and

Among the stone carvers posed on a massive pylon of the Lorain-Carnegie bridge, opened in 1932, was the father of noted comedian Bob Hope, for whom the bridge was later renamed. The Western Reserve Historical Society.

Shaker Heights) except the Germans, who had been integrated into the population "as evenly as the English, Welsh, Scotch, Irish, or Canadians." Cleveland's black population had increased considerably, from 34,451, or 4.3 percent of the city's population, in 1920, to 71,899, or 8 percent, in 1930. Cleveland's blacks lived in a section bounded by East 9th Street on the west, Euclid Avenue on the north, East 105th Street on the east, and, on the south, the tracks of the New York, Chicago & St. Louis Railroad just south of Woodland Avenue. There was also a small concentration of blacks living in the southwest section of the city along Bellaire Road between West 117th and West 130th streets, most of whom worked at the yards of the New York Central Railroad. Finally, some 1,200 blacks lived outside of Cleveland; these were largely house servants and chauffeurs living with their employers.

Cleveland's 394,898 gainful workers were employed largely in the manufacturing and mechanical industries (41 percent), trade (18 percent), domestic and personal service (10 percent), transportation and communication (11 percent), and the building industry (7 percent). Twenty percent worked in the service industries, including professional and semiprofessional service, public service, and domestic and personal service. Industries employing large numbers of Clevelanders in 1930 included (in round numbers) the building industry (28,000), blast furnaces and steel-rolling mills (19,000), other iron and steel industries (42,000), wholesale and retail trade (62,000), and steam railroads (15,000). Prophetically, one-seventh of Cleveland's gainful workers were out of work on the day in April 1930 preceding the visit of the census enumerator. (Nine months later, in January 1931, one-third would be out of work.)

By analyzing data for each census tract, Green statistically demonstrated for the first time in the city's history what he called the "great differences" among the economic areas within the five-city region of Cleveland, Lakewood, East Cleveland, Cleveland Heights, and Shaker Heights—differences in color, nativity, age, sex, literacy, employment, and the possession of radios and homes. Green identified fourteen "economic areas" by ranking each census tract according to "equivalent monthly rental." The results showed that a disparity in wealth between the city and the suburbs was already well established. Only 21 of Cleveland's 201 census tracts ranked within the seven highest economic areas (those paying $47 or more monthly rental), while all but 3 of the 51 census tracts outside of Cleveland ranked within the seven highest economic areas. "In the high economic areas," Green wrote, "the picture is quite different than in the low economic areas. Homes are owned, families have radios, family heads are native white of native parentage, illiteracy is low, unemployment is uncommon, population is spread out over ample areas, the juvenile delinquency rate is low, likewise the infant mortality rate and the general death-rate are low."

As early as 1930, census figures showed that Cleveland was "decaying at the core," with increases of population occurring on the periphery of the metropolitan area and decreases occurring at the center. So

Howard Whipple Green reported in the first *Real Property Inventory of Greater Cleveland*, published in 1933. The Real Property Inventory of Metropolitan Cleveland (RPI), of which Green served as director between 1932 and 1959, tracked movements of population into and out of census tracts in Greater Cleveland in the years between decennial census counts. Data of this kind, according to Green, were of great value for the "intelligent location and proper operation" of retail outlets, schools, branch banks, public transportation, and utilities. By charting trends, the RPI was designed to form the basis for "business judgments." In examining the periodic reports of the RPI over the city's long downward spiral, however, it becomes apparent that RPI not only charted trends but initiated them as well. Census Tract M-7 (bounded by East 55th and East 71st streets and Central and Quincy avenues) is a case in point. That neighborhood, centered at East 55th Street and Woodland Avenue, was home to large numbers of Russians, mostly Orthodox Jews, in 1920; ten years later, it was overwhelmingly black. "Few persons realized," Green wrote in the first edition of the RPI, "that census tract M-7 with 8.7% of its population Negro in 1920 would show 90.6% Negroes in 1930. An enormous increase in the number of Negroes in a particular section of the city with their influence on property values is always reflected sooner or later in mortgage finance."

By 1920, residential dispersion had already occurred among Cleveland's Irish and German populations. Between 1920 and 1930, once-strong enclaves of Italians and Russians living on the near East Side dispersed to other areas of the city and to the suburbs, while the black community became even more concentrated there, especially along Central and Scovill avenues. On the eve of the Depression, at least 90 percent of the city's blacks were concentrated in a ghetto bounded by Euclid and Woodland avenues and East 14th and East 105th streets.

The conditions of life of the typical black ghetto dweller were described by novelist Charles W. Chesnutt: "The majority live in drab, middle or low class houses, none too well kept up . . . while the poor live in dilapidated, rack-rented shacks, sometimes a whole family in one or two rooms, as a rule paying higher rent than white tenants for the same space." Despite these conditions, by most measures of socio-economic progress, the status of black migrants who came north after 1915 constituted an advance over their previous condition. In contrast to the 1960s, when Northern blacks were experiencing "actual gains but psychological losses" (as one sociologist has put it), blacks in Northern ghettos in the 1920s and 1930s recognized their improved status. Hence, Kenneth L. Kusmer has called this era the "Quiet Ghetto." Paradoxically, the consolidation of the ghetto after World War I produced a growing sense of black unity and a philosophy of self-help and race pride that would provide a basis for future struggle against racism in all its manifestations. And, as the black population spread eastward, gradually engulfing formerly white wards, the ghetto was transformed into an increasingly formidable political power.

In the months and years after the great stock market crash on Black Tuesday, 29 October 1929, Cleveland coasted downhill at dizzying speed. The economic and cultural preeminence of the previous decade reversed to a fight for survival in the 1930s. There were an estimated 41,000 jobless in Cleveland in April 1930, close to 100,000 by the following January. (In the Cleveland five-city area, the numbers were 44,000 and 106,000 respectively.) Economic dislocation reached enormous proportions. The expenditure of $200 million for direct and work relief in Cuyahoga County in the ten-year period 1928–1937 represented only one-sixth of the loss of $1.2 billion in normal wage and salary payments during the same period. According to one study, wages paid in industry in Cuyahoga County decreased from $251,942,813 in 1929 to $99,448,000 in 1933. To cope with rapidly shrinking tax revenues and the ever-growing need for massive amounts of direct relief (food, clothing, and shelter) to the unemployed, Mayor Ray T. Miller turned to the enforcement of strict economy in government. In 1931, $1 million was pared from municipal operating expenses and funneled to relief services, and a 1-mill county relief levy was adopted in 1932. But these measures fell far short of meeting the increasing cost of relief.

Within months of President Franklin Delano Roosevelt's inauguration, expanded federal assistance carried most of the relief burden. The Civil Works Administration (CWA), established in November

Cutbacks in the WPA program in the late 1930s led to protests such as these being staged by Cleveland women who had lost their WPA positions in 1939. Such cutbacks were made as the nation's economy began to improve. The Cleveland Press Collection, Cleveland State University.

1933, was followed by the Federal Emergency Relief Administration (FERA), which supplemented city, county, and state funds for direct relief and made work available to several thousand employable members of relief families. FERA's peak of activity in Cleveland occurred in July 1935, with 10,075 men and women on work relief. In 1935, care of the unemployable was given back to the Cuyahoga County Relief Administration, and the Work Progress Administration (later renamed the Work Projects Administration) was established to provide work relief for one employable member of each relief family. Statistics demonstrate the intensity of the need in Cleveland. The monthly average of those receiving direct and (after 1933) work relief rose from 3,499 in 1928 to 52,995 in 1933 and 77,565 in 1936. Expenditures for relief (exclusive of administration) rose from $1 million in 1928 to $14.5 million in 1933 and $39.8 million in 1936. The largest concentration of relief families and individuals, and the largest jobless ratios, were in those sections of the city Green had defined as "low economic areas" in 1930: the near West Side and the East Side south of Euclid Avenue. Suburban areas were much less hard hit. In describing the geographic distribution of relief families, Green illustrated the disparity in concrete terms: "Families in the low economic tenths have little; many are on relief and the others are on the edge of dependence. Families living in the highest economic tenth have much; they pay high rents, own expensive homes, have telephones, automobiles, mechanical refrigerators, and most that the heart desires." By March 1938, 54,849 residents of Cuyahoga County were receiving work relief under the CWA and the WPA. These programs carried on much of the area's capital improvements program, building streets, sewers, schools, and waterworks that would otherwise have been impossible. With aid from the WPA, the first portion of the lakefront highway (later called the Cleveland Memorial Shoreway) was built between East 9th Street and Gordon Park. In 1938–1939 the county, with WPA assistance, built the Main Avenue Bridge, which added another important high-level connection between the East and West sides of the city.

Cleveland's city and metropolitan parks especially benefited from the massive federal work projects. The Cleveland Metroparks System was substantially developed during this period with the construction of roads, trails, picnic areas, shelterhouses, and other structures. The *Cleveland Press* on 22 July 1936 commented that the improvements financed with federal dollars were sweeping Cleveland's metropolitan parks into a completed system "a generation ahead of schedule." The once-beautiful city parks, meanwhile, had suffered from three decades of inadequate maintenance, and many of the homeless were using them for sleeping quarters. In the late 1930s, WPA forces working two shifts extensively rehabilitated the parks and built new playgrounds. In a radio address in 1936, Parks Director Hugo E. Varga acknowledged that, without WPA help, "there would have been only a skeleton of the parks left as a bitter reminder of a penny-wise and pound-foolish policy. . . ." Another tangible legacy of work relief in

WPA programs put men to work on civic construction projects like this one at Brookside Park in 1938. The Cleveland Press Collection, Cleveland State University.

Cleveland was the art produced under the Public Works of Art Project and other programs that followed it. Unemployed Cleveland artists produced graphics, murals, paintings, and sculpture of exceptional quality and enjoyed warm public support. Much of the New Deal art exemplified the "Cleveland Scene," stressing pride in Cleveland's heritage—its people, industries, architecture, and accomplishments.

A significant revolution of the 1930s was the change in historical assumptions about social responsibility. Government recognized for the first time an obligation to provide decent housing for the poor, although the construction of public housing, at least initially, was primarily viewed as an emergency activity to put men to work. Under the leadership of Ernest J. Bohn, who served as the first director of the Cleveland Metropolitan Housing Authority, Cleveland led the nation in establishing the first public-housing projects to be funded by the Public Works Administration. Construction began on three PWA

Completed in 1939, the Lakeview Terrace public housing project re-placed a huddle of ramshackle dwellings on the west bank of the Cuya-hoga River. The project won national acclaim for its design. Ernest Bohn Collection, Case Western Reserve University.

projects in 1935: Cedar-Central Apartments, located between East 22nd and East 30th streets and Cedar and Central avenues; Outhwaite Homes, between East 40th and East 46th streets and Scovill and Woodland avenues; and Lakeview Terrace, at West 28th Street near the Main Avenue Bridge. The three projects, completed in 1937, provided apartments for 1,849 low-income families and resulted in the clearance of large slum areas. These were followed, in 1940, by Valley View Homes, at West 7th Street and Starkweather Avenue, and Woodhill Homes, at Woodhill Road and Woodland Avenue. (The latter used land formerly occupied by the popular amusement resort Luna Park.) All of the new housing projects were built in the modern functional style. One, Lakeview Terrace, received international recognition for its successful adaptation to a difficult site, its incorporation of the first community center in a public-housing project, and its use of the decorative arts, made possible by the Treasury Relief Art Project.

After Clevelanders voted to rescind the city manager plan and return to an elected mayor and ward councilmen in 1931, successive city administrations struggled to provide relief to the destitute. As the numbers on relief swelled beyond the ability of local social-welfare organizations to cope, the burden of caring for the poor and unemployed fell on the city, dooming Ray T. Miller to be a one-term mayor. Municipal government was in disarray under his successor, Harry L. Davis. City finances were in sad condition, and the police department was corrupt and demoralized. In 1935, Harold H. Burton was elected to the first of his three mayoral terms. By 1938, Burton had brought order to the city, balancing the budget and cleaning up the police department. To accomplish the latter, he brought in Eliot Ness, a young federal agent who had helped break the hold of the Capone mob in Chicago, to serve as safety director. Ness was given free rein to conduct investigations wherever he suspected corruption.

Iron and steel, and iron and steel products, remained the city's mainstay. The Republic Steel Corporation acquired Cleveland's Corrigan, McKinney Steel Company in 1935 and moved its headquarters from Youngstown to Cleveland. An improved economic outlook in 1936 encouraged Republic to undertake a major expansion of its Cleveland plant with the construction of a 98-inch continuous hot strip mill, then the widest in the world. The plant was repeatedly enlarged in the next three decades, and Republic, until 1980, remained Cleveland's largest single employer. The company weathered a difficult period of labor unrest in the 1930s, including the violent Little Steel Strike of 1937. Steelworkers failed to win union recognition, but several years later the federal government forced Republic to comply. Elsewhere, the Fisher Body Company and the Industrial Rayon Corporation were also the targets of serious strikes during this decade.

Signs of the changes to come in the city's commercial life occurred in the late 1920s and early 1930s with construction of the first major stores and shopping areas to be built outside of the downtown area. These included new Sears department stores on the East and West sides of the city (1928), the Shaker Square shopping center (1929), and branches of Bailey's department store at Euclid-East 105th and in Lakewood (1929–30). The Depression, then World War II, postponed further decentralization of the city's retail industry. The Depression sharply curtailed construction of all kinds, and, except for work-relief projects, few new buildings were erected in the 1930s. Two projects, however, would have a lasting impact on the city: Cleveland Municipal Stadium and the Great Lakes Exposition.

America in the 1920s was increasingly becoming a nation of spectators, and professional sports was becoming a popular and profitable activity. Other large cities, including Los Angeles, San Francisco, Chicago, and Baltimore, had built municipal stadiums, and Cleveland followed the trend. Promoted by City Manager William R. Hopkins, the new Municipal Stadium was seen as a fitting lakefront termination for the city's Group Plan. Voters approved a bond issue in 1928, and the Stadium made its debut in a program of song and speeches on 2 July 1931. The following year, on Sunday, 31 July 1932, the Cleveland Indians played their first game there. An astonishing 80,184 persons filled the ball park, and the next day's headlines captured the moment: "From Noon to 3 They Pour into Big Horseshoe through All Routes; Railroads Bring Thousands; Akron Sends 1,200; Same Number from Pittsburgh Area; 'Nap' Lajoie and Other Stars of Bygone Days Are Cheered; Depression Given Black Eye." Without a permanent lease, however, the Indians continued to play most of their games at League Park, in the Hough neighborhood, until 1947.

Another project helped revive a Depression-weary city. Business leaders planned the Great Lakes Exposition to celebrate the industry and culture of the eight Great Lakes states and the bordering provinces of Canada. The event also marked the centennial of Cleveland's incorporation as a city. The prospectus for the exposition summed up the important psychological benefits the event's promoters hoped for, stating, "Cleveland has for several years been so depressed by adverse circumstances that a forward-looking enterprise is needed to revive the sagging spirit of civic pride that formerly characterized the city." Financed by Cleveland business interests, the exposition ran from June through October over two years, 1936 and 1937. The lakefront exposition occupied the Mall from St. Clair Avenue north, and stretched from the Stadium to East 20th Street. Clevelanders witnessed the transformation of a former public dump into an attractively landscaped

Constructed on Cleveland's lakefront east of Municipal Stadium, the Great Lakes Exposition provided entertainment and lifted the spirits of Depression-weary Clevelanders in 1936 and 1937 while promoting business opportunities in the Great Lakes states. The Western Reserve Historical Society.

fairgrounds. The exposition offered exhibits of art, science, industry, and horticulture, as well as popular entertainment. Extensive use of light as an architectural element showed off Cleveland's prominence as a center of lighting-industry research. The Great Lakes Exposition advertised Cleveland as a progressive, productive city and pointed the way toward economic recovery. Among its lasting benefits was the final realization of the Group Plan; the last building remaining in the area designated for the Mall was removed in 1935.

Cleveland's cultural growth was seemingly unimpeded by the economic hardship of these years. The decade saw the founding of the Garden Center of Greater Cleveland in 1930 and the opening of Severance Hall, the new home of the Cleveland Orchestra, the following year. In 1936, Dunham Tavern, Inc., was organized to preserve the famous Euclid Avenue inn, and on 30 July 1939, 35,000 people representing 47 countries of origin attended the dedication of the Cleveland Cultural Gardens, which covered 35 acres in Rockefeller Park and paid tribute to the contributions of the city's diverse nationality groups.

Dorothea D. Kahn, staff correspondent of the *Christian Science Monitor*, visited Cleveland in late summer 1938. She found a city appealing "in spite of its bigness," a city struggling with a serious relief problem but blessed with business and civic leaders "striving with rolled up sleeves to solve the city's problems, to improve business and so make more jobs, to provide better public and private housing, to increase educational opportunities, and to beautify the city." Kahn saw massive downtown buildings, but few skyscrapers; an abundance of tree-shaded homes and new public-housing projects set down in slums; long viaducts that carried traffic high over the industrial valleys; and used-car lots with the legend "We finance WPA workers." Public Square gave the big industrial city a New England "common" for a center. There, statues of the city's heroes brought the past tangibly into the present; much more than in other cities, Kahn wrote, "you find yourself reminded of the men who made the city." Nearby, a newly made lakefront stretched out beyond the factories and industries that had formerly claimed the shore, and the Mall stood as "a symbol of the city's long and patient efforts to bring its ambitious plan to realization." While the gathering clouds of war in Europe would soon mean the revival of Cleveland's economy, the resulting lure of jobs would also transform the character of its population, accelerating the move to the suburbs and prompting the first uneasy feelings that something was wrong.

CHAPTER ELEVEN

War and Renewal

1940–1949

The Depression had brought Cleveland to its knees. Industrialist Cyrus Eaton would later say that Cleveland was hurt more by the Depression than any other city in the United States. That assertion, George Condon wrote in 1967, "is plausible enough to people who remember the exuberant, dynamic Cleveland of pre-Depression days and who can compare it with the somber, convalescent city that walked with a dragging gait and a querulous expression until recent years. The Cleveland that the world knew from 1930 to 1955 was a hurt town and it showed in many ways. There was a disposition toward petty bickering among the civic leaders over petty issues, while the large issue of Cleveland's future went untended and the sprawling downtown area turned gray and shabby." The period 1940–1949 was marked by war and postwar renewal, by personal sacrifice and industrial expansion that would carry over into a peacetime economy. Long before war's end, Cleveland would begin planning for its future, charting new highways and other improvements and considering, for the first time, the problem of interracial relations. Economic well-being—even victory in the 1948 World Series—seemed to give credence to the claim, born in this decade, that Cleveland was "the best location in the nation."

Cleveland in 1940 remained the nation's sixth-largest city, but for the first time its population count, 878,336, showed a small loss. Of that number, 20.4 percent were foreign-born white, while 10.0 percent were black. Outward migration to the suburbs had slowed during the Depression, and during World War II shortages of men and materials continued to discourage new construction of homes in outlying areas. But at war's end, pent-up demand was met with large new housing projects in such suburbs as Brooklyn, Lyndhurst, Mayfield Heights, Maple Heights, and South Euclid, and Cleveland would see no abatement of the trend for the duration of its modern history.

As the decade opened, Cleveland faced publicly for the first time the phenomenon of decentralization. A report published in 1941 by the Cleveland Chamber of Commerce stated frankly: "It is evident that most people who live in Cleveland are anxious to move to the suburbs. . . . Experience has shown that if their economic status permits, the majority of Clevelanders prefer to live outside the central area." The reasons for this preference, according to the report, were several, ranging from smoke and dirt to congestion, vice and crime, deterioration, and, finally, the "proximity of races having a depreciatory effect on values." Although Cleveland's population was again growing (as the 1950 census would show), the character of the city's inhabitants was changing. Native and foreign-born whites were leaving the city for the suburbs, and Appalachian whites and Southern blacks were arriving in large numbers to seek work in Cleveland's expanding wartime industries. At the same time, migrant workers from Puerto Rico began arriving in Cleveland. Large numbers of Appalachians and Puerto Ricans settled on the near West Side, and by 1970 some 20,000 Appalachians and 5,000 Puerto Ricans were living in that formerly Hungarian and Irish neighborhood. During the decade, Cleveland's black population grew from 85,000 to 148,000, and for the first time blacks began moving in substantial numbers into neighborhoods outside their traditional ghetto, including Hough, Mount Pleasant, Miles Heights, and Glenville. Glenville, annexed to Cleveland in 1905, was a predominantly Jewish neighborhood, many of whose residents had begun to move to Cleveland Heights when the first blacks moved there in the 1920s. Between 1940 and 1950, the black population in Glenville grew rapidly, from 1,069 to 20,517. In 1945, confronted by the problems of a changing neighborhood, residents formed the Glenville Community Council to address such areas of concern as interracial relations and the need for better recreational facilities, improved public safety, and stricter enforcement of the housing code. As early as 1945, Glenville's leaders recognized the presence of "potential powder kegs" in the crowded, changing neighborhood. Glenville was 67 percent black by 1960, and 95 percent black by the mid-1960s. The same pattern would occur again and again as white neighborhoods became black and segregation took hold of the city's East Side.

While suburban residents continued to shop, visit, find entertainment, and earn their livings in Cleveland, they did not share its responsibilities, and they contributed nothing to the support of its services. As Cleveland advertising executive and historian William Ganson Rose put it in 1950, the thriving cities and villages that "nestled close to the sprawling, fan-shaped mother city" were "content in their municipal independence and the charm of their residential sections." Civic and business leaders, meanwhile, struggled to find solutions to the population decline revealed in the 1940 census. Rose, at a meeting of the Greater Cleveland Council of Smaller Business of America, Inc., presented a program to counteract the alarming trend. He suggested that the city revise its zoning regulations, eliminate smoke nuisances and enforce sanitation laws, foster the renovation of buildings worthy of future use and get rid of unsafe and unfit structures, promote development by private investors of better neighborhoods, and encourage development of the lakeshore as a practical and pleasant place to live. Rose's program was the first of literally hundreds that would be put forward over the next four decades as the city struggled to reverse its decline.

Cleveland industries in the 1940s expanded rapidly to meet demand for war materiel. Cleveland factories turned out planes, tanks, trucks, jeeps, artillery and small arms, bombs, binoculars, and telescopes. Production at the Thompson Aircraft Products Company, a Defense Plant Corporation subsidiary, began in 1941. At Municipal Airport, the Fisher Aircraft Assembly Plant No. 2 was erected in 1942 for the assembly of B-29 bombers and, later, P-57 tanks. Nearby, the

Women, such as these at the Cleveland Cadillac Tank Plant in 1944, took on a large role in the city's industrial workforce during the man-power shortage of World War II. The Cleveland Press Collection, Cleveland State University.

$20-million National Advisory Committee for Aeronautics (NACA) Aircraft Engine Research Laboratory (later the NASA Lewis Research Center) opened in 1943.

Beginning with a national advertising slogan originated by the Cleveland Electric Illuminating Company in 1944 to help build post-war business, Cleveland claimed distinction as "the best location in the nation." The claim was based on the fact that within 500 miles of the city lived half the people of the United States and Canada; that Cleveland was the natural meeting place of iron ore, coal, copper, gyp-sum, stone, sand, and other vital raw materials; and that efficient water, rail, highway, and air transportation facilitated delivery and re-duced costs. As a leader in the lighting industry and an important producer of machine tools, electrical goods, metal products, and paints and varnish, Cleveland enjoyed a diversified industrial base, a large supply of trained workers, and abundant low-cost power and water. Northern Ohio, embracing the Cleveland, Lorain, and Youngstown districts, remained the steel center of the nation. A survey of occupations made in 1946 showed that out of a total employment of 560,000 in Cuyahoga County, four industrial groups predominated: machinery (66,000 workers), iron and steel (50,000), transportation equipment (34,000), and electrical machinery (26,000). But a measure of the diversity of Cleveland industry can be seen in the fact that, in 1944, the Cleveland Union Stockyards employed 4,000 workers, while the city's nine breweries employed more than 1,200. Industrial workers swelled the city's wartime population, and, at war's end, an already severe housing shortage worsened with the return of servicemen eager to start new families. Throughout the city, single-family homes were subdivided into units housing several families, beginning a pattern of overuse and overcrowding, and laying the groundwork for future deterioration.

In 1943, at a luncheon at the Statler Hotel, Mayor Frank J. Lausche organized the Postwar Planning Council to begin the work of preparing Cleveland for the end of war-contract production and to coordinate planning at all levels of community life. The aim of the council, which was financed by donations from business, industry, and labor, was, in Mayor Lausche's words, "not only to build the bridge from war to peacetime production but also to lay plans for making Cleveland's industrial advantages so patent that we can keep all of the industries we have and attract new ones. . . . " Cleveland was in a race with all other industrial cities, Lausche warned, and the days of rapid growth were over. Under Executive Director S. Burns Weston, five panels were named to study transportation, public works, interracial relations, the needs of returning servicemen, and public finance. Two panels deserve special mention. The role of the public-works panel was to stimulate public agencies to rush the production of construction plans. Interestingly enough, the freeway system was seen as the one public-works project that would absorb the first impact of the suspension of war work, and one of the panel's tasks was to

We can't fail them now!

GIVE! VICTORY CAMPAIGN
GREATER
CLEVELAND **WAR CHEST**
COMMUNITY FUND ★ WAR RELIEF ★ U.S.O.

During World War II, Cleveland's Community Fund supported not only local charities but organizations such as the U.S.O. (United Service Organization), which assisted servicemen and servicewomen. The Cleveland Public Library.

spur planning and land acquisition "mercilessly" (as a *Cleveland Press* reporter put it). A panel on interracial relations, chaired by Dr. Leonard Mayo, dean of the School of Applied Social Sciences of Western Reserve University, was charged with answering the question: Are the community and its facilities prepared to deal objectively with interracial relations? The panel defined areas where problems existed—such as housing, recreation, health, and employment practices—and recommended that the mayor follow a policy of preventive action rather than wait for problems to come to a head. As a result of the panel's work, the Cleveland Community Relations Board was established in 1945, with a mission "to promote amicable relations among the racial and cultural groups within the community."

During the late 1940s, Mayor Thomas A. Burke initiated the first major municipal projects since the erection of Cleveland Stadium in 1930–1931. The popular Burke, who served as mayor for nine years (1945–1953), sponsored construction of the downtown airport and activated the dormant plan, first conceived by the Van Sweringens, for a system of rapid-transit lines serving Cleveland. In 1942, the city of Cleveland, with some reluctance, had acquired the near-bankrupt Cleveland Railway Company, thereby becoming the owner and operator of a street railway system with 4,400 employees and an annual business of $15 million. The new Cleveland Transit System, under the supervision of the city's public utilities department, made the transition from streetcars to buses and completed construction of a new 19-mile rapid-transit system in 1955. The line extended from Windermere Station near Euclid and Superior avenues on the East Side to West 140th Street and Lorain Avenue. An additional link to the airport, completed in 1968, gave Cleveland the first rapid-transit system in the country providing a direct rail connection between the downtown business district and the airport.

In February 1944, a master freeway plan was completed by the Express Highway Subcommittee of the Regional Association of Cleveland. The plan followed on the heels of a freeway program and bond issue of $4.5 million endorsed by the voters four years earlier but delayed by war and the lack of a comprehensive plan. The plan called for a $240-million integrated freeway system as the solution to metropolitan Cleveland's traffic problems. While the plan bears striking similarity to the freeway system as built—it shows, for example, an inner belt, the Willow Freeway (I-77), an outer belt (I-271), and an outer belt south (I-480)—the differences are notable. The West Shoreway, following the lakefront as far as Rocky River, forms the major east-west highway on the West Side, not I-90, while the Berea-Airport Freeway (I-71), as planned, followed a substantially different route from that built. Finally, the proposed Medina, Newburgh, and Heights freeways were never built, though not until the 1970s were

The construction of freeways, such as Interstate 71, permitted Clevelanders to live at great distances from their jobs in the city. As shown in this view, the highways often cut neighborhoods in two. The Cleveland Public Library.

the latter two projects finally scrapped. In addition to freeways, other major public-works projects were under way. By the mid-1940s, substantial progress had been made on improving the Cuyahoga River for navigation; plans called for widening, straightening, and deepening the river channel. The city's stock of public housing was enlarged with the extension of Outhwaite Homes and the construction of Carver Park, the latter consisting of 1,287 units at Unwin Road near Central Avenue and East 43rd Street.

Superficially at least, Cleveland was healthy during these years. Clevelanders had generously supported the war effort. The temporary War Service Center on Public Square, whose walls carried the names of local men who had died in service to their country, represented the volunteer efforts of Clevelanders and was an active center for recruitment and the sale of war bonds. Alexander Winton's pioneer automobile, built in 1896, and the Brush dynamo that gave the city electric light in 1893 at a plant on Lime Street were both donated for their scrap value, and victory gardens were planted throughout the city. The existence of racial tensions had been acknowledged and the first steps taken to ease them. The Cleveland Convention and Visitors Bureau reported that conventions brought 152,185 visitors to Cleveland during 1946. The same year, Bill Veeck purchased the Cleveland Indians and subsequently orchestrated the liveliest and most memorable period in Cleveland baseball history. Throughout 1946, Clevelanders celebrated the city's 150th birthday with pageants, parades, and entertainment, drawing national attention. L. H. Robbins, in the *New York Times Magazine*, commented favorably on the city and its people: "Clevelanders display an exuberant enthusiasm for their town and their way of life such as you don't recall ever noting in any city east of the Alleghenies. . . . It really is remarkable, their town-boosting, their local pride and contentment. . . . " Robbins reported on the city's industrial might (noting that the Terminal Tower was "blacked out, some days, in the smoke pall from the valley") and its fine public buildings ("Here is a civic center to shout about"), though he acknowledged that, beyond the downtown core, "the first miles aren't so good."

Indeed, there were signs of trouble ahead. Within the city, as Mayor Lausche noted in his speech launching the Postwar Planning

Council, were slums with "living conditions unfit for human beings."
The city had expanded carelessly, and the mansions that remained on
Millionaires' Row (Euclid Avenue) rubbed shoulders with billboards
and car-wash lots, tourist homes and factories. Metropolitan progress,
many thought, was hampered by the disintegration of government into
more than one hundred independent taxing units. Above all, decentralization was accelerating. Of $1.7 billion spent on postwar indus-
trial expansion, one billion was spent in the suburbs. Of the resulting
170,000 new job opportunities, the suburbs got 100,000, the central
city 70,000. And suburban home construction was outpacing home
construction in the city four to one. "Every metropolitan area is
plagued by the paradox of suburbs siphoning off tax income," *Architectural Forum* would comment in 1955. "In Cleveland this parasitic situation reaches an extreme. . . . Suburban chauvinism in Cleveland
is more than a political and financial problem. It is a social problem."
The problem, in coming years, would only worsen.

CHAPTER TWELVE

Exodus and Decline

1950–1965

Cleveland, in the early 1950s, stood at a crossroads. Its central business district and its neighborhoods were deteriorating. Crime was worsening, and thousands of city residents were leaving for new homes in the suburbs. Over the next fifteen years, civic and business leaders would struggle to define the problem, but answers would remain elusive. Urban renewal and the construction of freeways, meanwhile, would dramatically and permanently change the face of the city. And, while the Erieview plan would serve as a critical catalyst for future downtown renewal, the city's single-minded focus on the central business district would lead eventually to conflagration in Hough and yet another turning point in Cleveland's history.

Recognition that something was wrong unfolded gradually. In a speech to the Rotary Club in March 1953, Elmer L. Lindseth, president of the Illuminating Company, named some of the issues the city faced. These included downtown decay (no new office buildings had been built since the Terminal group); slum areas and areas that threatened to become slums ("in some cases only for lack of enforcing our building codes"); inadequate transportation and parking; and a need for affordable private housing and new schools, parks, and hospital beds. On 13 October 1954, city leaders met at the Mid-Day Club to map strategies for making the downtown more attractive to shoppers; according to the next day's account of the meeting in the *Plain Dealer*, no one mentioned the huge new shopping centers that had been built on the periphery of "Greater" Cleveland. Several months later, in a front-page story, the newspaper asked: Is Cleveland's downtown district dying? Blight, it said, had settled on "whole chunks" of the downtown, including the old wholesale district northwest of the Public Square and East 9th Street, the downtown's major north-south artery; retail sales in the central business district had failed to follow the upward curve of Greater Cleveland's growth in population and prosperity; and parking adjacent to Euclid Avenue was scarce. Yet, the paper reported, many businessmen believed the heart of Cleveland was strong compared with the downtowns of other large American cities, and that some postwar developments—for example, new access routes such as the East Shoreway, Chester Avenue, and the Willow Freeway; express buses, which had replaced streetcars; and the CTS Rapid Transit and Innerbelt Freeway (both under construction)—had contributed to the health and prosperity of downtown Cleveland. *Plain Dealer* editor Philip Porter has called this period in Cleveland's life the era of "coasting," of "abnormal goodwill." Industry appeared healthy, and the "Best Location" slogan was adopted enthusiastically by the newspapers and the Chamber of Commerce. Democrat Anthony J. Celebrezze, Cleveland's first five-term mayor (1954–1962), presided over much of the period. He maintained a minimum level of city services while keeping taxes low and, under urban renewal, oversaw sweeping changes downtown and in other areas of the city.

As a result of wartime in-migration, Cleveland's population in 1950 showed a small increase of 4.2 percent—up from 878,336 to 914,808. But Cuyahoga County population continued to increase at a much faster rate, so that slightly more than one-third (34 percent) of the county's population now lived outside of Cleveland. The foreign-born represented a decreasing proportion of the city's population in 1950 (15 percent, compared to 20 percent a decade earlier), blacks an increasing proportion (16 percent, compared to 10 percent in 1940). While the cities of Cleveland, Cleveland Heights, East Cleveland, and Lakewood all showed small increases in population, eight cities had

Erieview, centered around East 9th Street, was the city's major urban renewal effort in the 1960s. The first major structure to be completed was the Erieview Tower (1964). The Cleveland Public Library.

increased by more than 100 percent: Brooklyn (552 percent), Lynd-hurst (240 percent), Mayfield Heights (193 percent), Maple Heights (181 percent), South Euclid (166 percent), Euclid (147 percent), Parma (141 percent), and Fairview Park (123 percent). Postwar pros-perity, the construction of new highways, and the ready availability of low-cost, federally insured mortgages all accelerated the move to the suburbs. Racial transition in many of the city's East Side neighbor-hoods was another major factor in the unprecedented white flight that took place during this period. Fortunes were made by blockbusting, a tactic the city's Community Relations Board was hard-pressed to stop. In poorer neighborhoods, large single-family houses were subdi-vided and, as rental income dwindled, often no longer maintained.

Dramatic and rapid changes in the city's neighborhoods were accompanied by similarly dramatic and rapid growth in formerly rural areas outside the city's borders. Perhaps the most phenomenal change occurred in Parma, which grew from 28,000 in 1950 to 82,000 in 1960.

Retail stores followed the exodus. Prior to 1940, Shaker Square was the only shopping center in Cuyahoga County resembling the modern integrated centers of today. Developed by the Van Sweringens, it incorporated off-street parking, even though very limited by later standards. Suburban shopping centers mushroomed after World War II. Among these were Van Aken-Warrensville (Shaker Heights) in 1947; Eastgate (Mayfield Heights) and Westgate (Fairview Park) in 1954; Southgate (Maple Heights) in 1955; Parmatown (Parma) in 1956; and Golden Gate (Mayfield Heights) in 1958. Large suburban shopping centers evolved into climate-controlled regional malls, usually with two full-line department stores serving as anchors at either end. The first shopping mall in the Cleveland area, Severance Center, opened in Cleveland Heights in 1963.

While these suburban centers drained income from retail sales from the city center, Cleveland remained a powerful industrial center during these years. In 1950, 42 percent of Clevelanders who worked were engaged in manufacturing. The *Cleveland Press* (27 January 1953) announced that 1952 had been one of the best business years of all time; 101 new manufacturing concerns were established, and existing industries spent more than $146 million for expansion and new equipment. Cleveland looked forward to completion of the St. Lawrence Seaway, anticipating that it would restore the city to a position of prominence as a port of general commerce and create a new wave of industrial growth as manufacturers sought dockside locations to cash in on the lowest shipping and handling rates in history. An $8-million bond issue to improve port facilities was approved in 1955. In anticipation of 1959, when the Seaway was to open, the Cleveland area's development potential looked promising. It was located in a favorable market; it enjoyed unlimited water resources, abundant electric power, a good labor reservoir, and an unexcelled combination of transportation facilities; raw materials were near at hand. "New Era of Prosperity on the Way," read the headline in the special Cleveland supplement to the European edition of the *New York Herald Tribune* published in March 1956.

Coincident with postwar industrial expansion was the implementation of two federal programs that would have a profound impact not only on Cleveland but also on virtually all large American cities: the Housing Act of 1949, which established the federal urban-renewal program, and the Federal Highway Act of 1956, which gave impetus to a nationwide network of freeways by providing federal funding for 90 percent of construction costs. The concept of urban renewal was simple: Using its power of eminent domain if necessary, the city purchased property in specific project areas that had been legislatively determined as blighted. The property was cleared and improved for redevelopment, then sold to private developers at a reduction (called a writedown) from its assembly cost. The federal government absorbed two-thirds of the net project cost. Until 1950, Cleveland—"with slums as vast and as wretched as are to be found anywhere in the country," according to the *Plain Dealer* (16 April 1954)—had relied exclusively on the construction of public housing as a means of fighting blight. It had built eight developments, with 5,179 units providing housing for 18,951 low-income persons. Urban renewal was seen as a solution to the problem of multiple ownerships in blighted areas and the high cost of assembling sites for new, large-scale redevelopment.

In March 1955, residents living on East 38th Street between Scovill and Woodland avenues were invited to witness demolition of the first house—at 2534 East 38th Street—signaling the redevelopment of "Area B" (later called Longwood) and the start of urban renewal in Cleveland. By June 1958, 800 new dwelling units, new streets, and a playground had been built there, making it one of the first housing projects completed under urban renewal in the United States. The next target, "Area C" (St. Vincent Center), was less successful. Launched in 1959, Cleveland's biggest urban-renewal project to date encompassed 114 acres between East 19th and East 33rd streets and Woodland and Central avenues. Deteriorated buildings housing some 1,800 families (95 percent nonwhite, 98 percent tenants) were demolished; new apartments housing up to 3,500 middle-income families were to be built in their place. No developers came forward, however, and in 1963, Redevelopment Director James M. Lister acknowledged that there was no longer a market for the kind of housing that had been envisioned.

The urban-renewal program in Cleveland, encompassing just over 6,000 acres, was the largest in the country. Seven inner-city areas, all on the East Side, were targeted for urban renewal: Garden Valley, Longwood, East Woodland, University-Euclid, St. Vincent Center, Gladstone, and Erieview. Ultimately, residential projects (Garden Valley, Longwood, University-Euclid) were able to attract only developers of government-subsidized housing, and, although Garden Valley was acclaimed as "one of the boldest and most imaginative redevelopment jobs conceived in any city," by 1963 occupancy had reached only about

St. Theodosius Russian Orthodox Cathedral on Starkweather Road in the Tremont neighborhood forms a backdrop for Cleveland's Valleyview public housing facility in 1940. Ernest Bohn Collection, Case Western Reserve University.

50 percent and the Garden Valley Housing Association had defaulted on its mortgage. The East Woodland and Gladstone project areas, targeted for industrial reuse, actually experienced *declines* in assessed value from prerenewal levels, as did St. Vincent Center, which stood largely vacant until Cuyahoga Community College was planned in the late 1960s. Only Erieview was successful in attracting substantial new private investment.

A significant lesson from Cleveland's urban-renewal experience was the difficulty of creating effective demand for land in the inner city. Residents in these areas lacked adequate income to support new residential redevelopment without heavy subsidies, while industries often preferred to locate in suburban areas, near freeways and, usually, closer to their employees' homes. Further, the large-scale dispersal of the city's poorest residents naturally had major consequences for the adjoining neighborhoods that absorbed them. By 1958, city council members were voicing their concerns about the effects of displaced slum dwellers in the Hough, Glenville, Mount Pleasant, and upper Central areas. In addition to urban renewal, the construction of highways, facilitated by the Federal Highway Act of 1956, caused significant alterations in traditional land-use patterns. The network of freeways led first to the massive dispersal of population and demolition of housing, followed by the movement of commercial and industrial activities to the periphery of the city. By 1975, the interstate highway system had displaced an estimated 19,000 Clevelanders, resulting in significant losses not only of people but of income and property taxes as well.

Spurred by the availability of urban-renewal funds, planning thrived in Cleveland during these years. The City Planning Commission, under the direction of John T. Howard, had issued the General Plan of 1949 laying out general guidelines for the growth and development of the city. The downtown was expected to continue as the "natural" main business and shopping area, and the freeway plan of 1944 was made an integral part of the plan. Ten years later, the commission issued another plan, soon superseded by Erieview, called "Downtown Cleveland 1975." Envisioned was the virtual reorganization and redevelopment of the downtown, including the redesign of Public Square and Playhouse Square, and the construction of a subway under Euclid Avenue between East 14th Street and the Terminal.

By the mid-1950s, many of the institutions at University Circle had embarked on large expansion programs. The University Circle Development Foundation (later University Circle, Inc.) was created in 1957 to reinforce the commitment of cultural institutions to the Circle and to implement a twenty-year development plan. The plan proposed the creation of a "unified, beautiful, cultural center" and called for development of parking, new roadways, a shuttle-bus service, and a private police force. The ambitious plans also called for massive demolition—including a great deal of what Eric Johannesen would later call the "architectural museum" that constituted Magnolia Drive and other streets in the historic Wade Park area—much of which was later tempered by the economic constraints of the late 1960s and the 1970s. Many other plans, public and private, were frustrated and eventually abandoned because of a lack of money. Plans formulated between 1944 and 1967 for the city's near West Side called for commercial revitalization by creating new parking lots, traffic arteries, and "open space." Planners often assumed that such low-income areas were "blighted" and, in some cases, recommended wholesale demolition. The City Planning Commission in 1944 and again in 1961 recommended major redevelopment of the near West Side. Voters in 1963 rejected an $8-million urban-renewal bond issue that would have resulted in demolition of substantial portions of the neighborhood between West 25th and West 58th streets. Still another plan, in 1967, recommended the total clearance of what only a few years later would become the core of the Ohio City restoration effort.

The Erieview plan of 1960 was one of the nation's most ambitious urban-renewal plans. Prepared for the city by the internationally known firm of I. M. Pei & Associates, the plan called for clearance of the aging district northeast of downtown to provide sites for the construction of new office buildings, hotels, and housing. Erieview, it was hoped, would generate interest with the incentives provided by the urban-renewal program and encourage new private capital investment. Erieview embraced 163 acres located between East 6th and East 17th streets and between Chester Avenue and the lakefront. Almost

75 percent of the buildings in the project area were determined to be substandard; these and others that did not conform to the proposed plan were acquired and demolished. Parcels of land were assembled and gradually sold to private developers at substantial discounts. Erieview Tower, a forty-story office building at the heart of the project area, was erected first. The green glass curtain-wall building, incorporating a large plaza and reflecting pool, was completed in 1964 and served as a dramatic symbol of the entire redevelopment effort. Interestingly, it was built by a Columbus developer, John W. Galbreath; no Cleveland firm was prepared to take the risk. A dozen other large buildings, private and public, followed over the next two decades. Among these were One Erieview Plaza (1965), the Federal Building (1967), the Bond Court Building (1971), the Public Utilities Building (1971), and Park Centre (1973). The latter consisted of two twenty-story apartment buildings and a two-story shopping mall. By 1972, over $220 million of construction had been committed to the Erieview project, and the following decade would see the construction of many other large projects, including two new hotels, and the firm establishment of a new office and financial district with East 9th Street as its spine.

Erieview was not without its critics. Philip Porter called it "the mistake that ruined downtown." Erieview, Porter contended, "was no slum," and its redevelopment accelerated the deterioration of Euclid Avenue as Cleveland's major shopping street by draining it of people. Others criticized Erieview for producing a boring consistency and for eliminating the color, variety, and continuity that give a city character. But Erieview attracted critical new private investment, and without it, the construction of new office space might have followed the flight to the suburbs. As one city planner put it in 1972, Erieview "could be viewed as the catalyst which pulled the downtown area out of an otherwise inevitable downward spiral." In future years, Erieview would accommodate the expansion of Cleveland's service economy and point the way toward development of the lakefront. Nevertheless, from the perspective of the 1960s, one criticism remains valid: Erieview during this period claimed all of the city's energy and attention, while other parts of the city were generally neglected.

As Erieview made slow but sustained progress, yet another plan to "save" downtown Cleveland was unveiled in 1965. The two-year, $150,000 study was made by the firm of Ernst & Ernst at the behest of the Cleveland Development Foundation. It offered recommendations to speed Cleveland's rebirth and called for, among other things, a dizzying program of new construction: 5,500 to 6,600 new residential units, 2,300 new hotel rooms, and 12,000 new parking spaces in multilevel garages by 1975; and 5,000 additional residential units, 900 additional hotel rooms, and 9,000 additional parking spaces by 1985. Noting that "Cleveland has serious problems with its image and business climate," Ernst & Ernst partner Kenneth C. Caldwell reported that in the seven years since 1958, employment downtown had dropped from 125,000 to 116,000, and retail sales had declined by $52 million. The number of convention delegates was also down. On the eve of the Hough Riots, the city's focus remained firmly fixed on the downtown.

CHAPTER THIRTEEN

The Loss of Confidence
1966–1979

Though the fountains on the Mall, a gift of the Leonard C. Hanna Fund, were turned on in August 1964; though the new $17.5-million underground Convention Center was opened that month with the "Parade of Progress" showing off the best of the city's industry and technology, commerce, science, arts, and education; though Erieview was giving Cleveland a new physical image and Clevelanders a sense of pride and success some thought no longer possible—these signs of well-being were illusory. For, as business and civic leaders focused on the rebirth of downtown Cleveland, the city's neighborhoods were in disarray. Nowhere was that more apparent than in Hough. Bounded by Superior and Euclid avenues and by East 55th and East 105th streets, Hough had changed from a middle- to a working-class neighborhood beginning in the 1940s. In 1950, its two square miles were home to 66,000 Clevelanders, 95 percent of whom were white. Many of the neighborhood's large houses had been subdivided into three or four units, and landlords routinely ignored housing-code violations. A neighborhood conservation drive launched in 1951 by the Hough Area Council targeted the problems of architectural eyesores, ill-run taverns, crime, and, later, blockbusting. During this decade, blacks displaced by urban renewal began moving to Hough, and by 1960 the neighborhood was 74 percent black. Four years later, the county welfare department opened its first neighborhood office in Hough, where 25 percent of welfare cases now lived. In a series of articles in February 1965, the *Cleveland Press* warned that Hough was "in crisis." Two months later, it reported insurance cancellations there because of widespread vandalism and arson. Meanwhile, progress in the University-Euclid urban-renewal project, launched in 1960, was dismal. University-Euclid was to have created a new model community and rehabilitated more than 1,400 existing homes in eastern Hough; instead, it was the nightmare of Cleveland's urban-renewal program. By 1965, almost $7 million had been spent, with very little to show for it.

Frustration was mounting. Mayor Ralph S. Locher and other city leaders could not or would not see the trouble brewing despite sporadic outbreaks of violence during the early part of the summer of 1966. Roving gangs were harassing drivers and hurling rocks and bottles at businesses and passing vehicles on Superior Avenue. A brief, uneasy lull was broken on Monday night, 18 July, by an outbreak of violence that would last for four days and result in the deaths of four blacks and millions of dollars of damage to property. Mayor Locher described the East Side rioting as a "tragic day in the life of our city." The jeeps of the National Guard lining the major arteries shocked the white community out of its complacency. The mood of the city was one of fear and futility. The city whose vision had once made it a national leader now faced staggering losses on all sides. Over the next fifteen years, Cleveland would struggle to regroup and survive.

In the space of a few years, it seemed, the fabric of the city, both physically and psychologically, was shredded. The much-vaunted Cleveland public school system was declining. Department stores—among them William Taylor, Bailey's, and Sterling-Lindner—were closing, as were the theaters at Playhouse Square. Cleveland was losing population and jobs. The heaviest job losses were in manufacturing, once the city's mainstay. Formerly sound neighborhoods, now the province of the poor, deteriorated rapidly, and on streets where people had once lived and shopped, only rows of empty, gutted buildings remained. The city was hard-pressed to provide even a minimum level

National Guard troops stand ready to patrol Cleveland's East Side during the Hough Riots of 1966. The Cleveland Press Collection, Cleveland State University.

of service. Crime increased, vacant lots became dumping grounds, and the empty hulks of heavy industry were bitter reminders of a prosperous past. Cleveland was an aging city where nothing seemed to go right, where even the river caught fire: Cleveland not only shared America's urban crisis, it epitomized it.

The Cleveland Little Hoover Commission, formed in December 1965 to make an in-depth study of all city operations, submitted its reports in the aftermath of the Hough riots. It identified community relations as the city's "No. 1 problem." The commission was also extremely critical of the police department—which it called "defensive, isolated, parochial, and mistrustful of the public it serves"—and of the department's program of race relations, giving credence to long-standing complaints by blacks of unfair treatment. Though most of the problems had their roots long before Locher took office, he bore the blame. The newspapers turned on him—"Locher has had little or no rapport with that third of his city's population that is Negro," the *Plain Dealer* charged—and sought a replacement.

Many in Cleveland looked to State Representative Carl B. Stokes as "insurance" against further racial disorder, and as someone to give the city a chance to move forward again. In 1967, the eyes of the nation were on Cleveland as Stokes narrowly defeated Republican Seth Taft to become the first black mayor of a major U.S. city. Only seven months after Stokes took office, however, Cleveland police and black militants clashed in Glenville. A shoot-out on 23 July 1968 left ten dead and dozens wounded. By daybreak, the Ohio National Guard was mobilized to arrest widespread sniping, looting, and arson. The Glenville shoot-out killed much of Stokes's support. Corporate Cleveland had supported a major Stokes initiative, the Cleveland: NOW! campaign, which collected money and channeled it into myriad improvement projects of Stokes's choosing. When Cleveland: NOW! money was later traced to Fred (Ahmed) Evans, the central figure in the Glenville shoot-out, donations plummeted. The predominantly white police force became Stokes's bitter foe, and racial division deepened throughout the city. Stokes and city council president James Stanton battled each other over virtually every issue. The newspapers got tough on Stokes. Later, in his autobiography, *Promises of Power* (1973), Stokes railed against their "simple-minded" interpretation that, "if only we could put our personalities and our vanities in the background and get along, the city could move ahead." In fact, Stokes wrote, he and Stanton were diametrically opposed on important issues—public housing, equal employment opportunity, gun control—on which there was no middle ground. Although Stokes managed to win reelection to a second term, he lost the support of many of his original backers and, tired of strife with the city council, chose not to run for a third term.

Cleveland had been losing population since 1950, but the exodus accelerated dramatically after 1960, and by the early 1970s the rate of loss had climbed to some 20,000 persons a year. At the same time, the county outside of Cleveland continued to grow, though at a slower

Carl B. Stokes, who would go on to become the first black mayor of a major American city, debates opponent Seth Taft at the City Club of Cleveland during the 1967 mayoral campaign. The Cleveland Press Collection, Cleveland State University.

rate, until the 1980 census confirmed that it, too, was losing population.

	Cleveland	Cuyahoga County	City as % of County
1950	914,808	1,389,532	66%
1960	876,050	1,647,895	53%
1970	750,879	1,720,835	44%
1980	573,822	1,498,400	38%

As the city's population declined, the proportion of its black population rose dramatically, from 16 percent in 1950 to 38 percent in 1970 and 44 percent in 1980. The city was not only losing residents but also retaining a more dependent population. On the average, Cleveland residents were significantly poorer than the area's suburban population: in 1969, the average income for all city families ($9,717) was almost $6,000 below that for suburban families ($15,259), according to City Planning Commission statistics. Almost one-third of the city's families lived in substandard housing. By 1970, abandonment of entire neighborhoods—a phenomenon concentrated in all-black neighborhoods with high poverty and crime rates—was well under way and spreading. Between 1966 and 1974, the city spent over $4 million on the demolition of abandoned buildings and still could not keep pace with abandonment, which was estimated at three units per day. A Brookings Institution study in 1975 ranked Cleveland second among fifty-eight big cities having the worst social and economic problems. (Only Newark, New Jersey, ranked worse.)

Meanwhile, regional shifts confirmed that the city was becoming a less viable location for many kinds of economic activity. Although Cleveland's central business district was expanding as an office center, it lost dominance as a shopping center as its share of retail sales and employment declined. Vacant stores, however, were a citywide phenomenon: Real Property Inventory field counts showed that the number of occupied store units in Cleveland decreased from 15,768 in 1958 to 12,269 in 1972. The rest of the county, meanwhile, had gained store units: from 5,137 in 1958 to 6,735 in 1972. Many industries were abandoning obsolete, multistory buildings for modern one-story plants in the suburbs, usually on or near the freeway. The case of the National Screw & Manufacturing Company was typical. National Screw, a leader in the fastener industry, had occupied a large multistory plant at East 75th Street and Stanton Avenue since 1889. In the 1940s, it produced more than fifty thousand different items; in 1936, the plant's amateur women's softball and bowling teams both won national championships. But in 1969, National Screw moved to a more efficient one-story plant in Mentor, taking with it more than a thousand jobs. The abandoned plant, empty and gutted, remained a startling sight for years, and a frequent target for arson. Between 1958 and 1977, Cleveland lost an estimated 130,000 jobs, while the suburbs of Cuyahoga County gained almost 210,000. By 1970, slightly more than half of all jobs in the Cleveland Standard Metropolitan Sta-

These views, taken in 1933 and 1976, graphically depict the fate of the National Screw & Manufacturing plant at East 75th Street and Stanton Avenue after the company left Cleveland in 1969. The Cleveland Press Collection, Cleveland State University.

tistical Area (Cuyahoga, Medina, Lake, and Geauga counties) were located in the suburbs. Many heavy industries, however, were leaving the region altogether, choosing to relocate to the Sun Belt or abroad, where wages and other costs were substantially lower. The bulk of the losses occurred in the durable-goods (metals) sector. Richard B. Tullis, president of the Harris-Intertype Corporation, in 1972 told the *Plain Dealer* that Cleveland would have to face up to the inevitable trend of major industries being replaced by light manufacturing and service industries.

The early 1970s were sad, tumultuous years for Cleveland, years when the city seemed to be in the midst of its own Great Depression, years of physical and psychological erosion. The parks were, once again, dumping grounds. The transit system was approaching finan-

cial disaster. The downtown, offering little to attract people, was largely dead at night, and the opening of the Coliseum in Richfield (Summit County) in 1974 further drained it of life while making it more difficult for Clevelanders to support the home teams. To outsiders, Cleveland was the butt of jokes on TV's "Laugh-In," the "mistake-on-the-lake."

Two projects that would later prove important to the city's well-being had their start in these years. By the late 1960s, modest efforts were under way to make the Flats, site of the city's earliest industries, the center of Cleveland nightlife. The *Cleveland Press* recognized this trend in 1968 when it wrote: "There is a bit of the romantic down there. . . , with the rough and tumble seamen's bars, the cobblestone streets and the old buildings reeking [of] Cleveland's history." Settlers' Landing, a project of the Higbee Company, envisioned a complex of shops, restaurants, and entertainment facilities near the traditional landing site of city founder Moses Cleaveland. Though that project failed, it succeeded in focusing attention on the waterfront, and by the mid-1970s an informal coalescing of bars, restaurants, and shops—many occupying former industrial buildings—had infused the area with new life.

The historic-preservation movement began to make modest gains during this period. Particularly notable were the efforts of Ray K. Shepardson, who conceived the idea of saving the old movie and vaudeville palaces at Playhouse Square which had been for decades the center of the city's nightlife. The Playhouse Square Association was organized in 1970. With support from the Junior League and other volunteers, the association created a cabaret theater in the lobby of the State Theater. The production of *Jacques Brel Is Alive and Well and Living in Paris* captured the public imagination and helped launch a concerted effort to preserve the theaters and restore them to their former glory. There were other, small signs of downtown renewal. Lunchtime concerts on the Mall and at Huron Road Mall and Chester Commons (a new vest-pocket park of above-average design) drew thousands, while weekly "parties in the park," sponsored by the Greater Cleveland Growth Association, helped keep young adults downtown after work and boost business at Cleveland restaurants and nightclubs.

Planning continued during these years, although it took a new tack. Between 1969 and 1979, under the direction of Norman Krumholz, the City Planning Commission worked to achieve what it called "equity objectives." Recognizing that Cleveland was not only losing population but also retaining a more dependent population, the commission staff deemphasized planners' traditional concerns with zoning, land use, and urban design and instead focused on plans and issues aimed at ameliorating the worst problems of the city and its residents. The planning commission, for example, championed the needs of the transit-dependent (a 1969 survey showed that one-third of Cleveland's families had no automobile), securing reduced fares and service guarantees during the negotiations that led to the transfer of the Cleveland Transit System to the Greater Cleveland Regional Transit Authority in 1975. Under three mayors who could not have been more different (Carl Stokes, Ralph J. Perk, and Dennis Kucinich), Krumholz continued to urge that the city abandon its preoccupation with what urbanologist Jane Jacobs had called "cataclysmic change" and focus instead on strategies aimed at conservation and gradual improvement.

In the 1970s, Cleveland, like many other of the nation's ailing cities that found themselves competing for new development, offered public subsidies to stimulate the private real-estate market. It was hoped that property-tax abatement would lure investors, and thereby create jobs. Under Mayor Ralph Perk, the National City Bank Building was built, and Stouffer's Inn on the Square renovated, with the aid of tax abatement. A growing number of critics, however, claimed that the projects would have been built without tax abatement, and that such public largess served only to further erode the city's tax base. In 1975, the city of Cleveland, the Greater Cleveland Growth Association, and the Cleveland Foundation together commissioned Lawrence Halprin & Associates of San Francisco to develop a plan to rejuvenate the downtown. Following a series of public workshops, Halprin unveiled his "Concept for Cleveland." It offered few ideas that went beyond the obvious and clichéd responses to "urban blight." Among the recommendations was the creation of a pedestrian mall on Euclid Avenue. Some of the plans—open trolleys, for example, and sidewalk cafes— failed to account for the Cleveland climate, while others—the depression of Superior Avenue underground and reconstruction of Public Square above it—failed to respect the city's historical sense of place. In a page-one editorial, the *Plain Dealer* praised the plan for its "color, pizzazz, magnetism, [and] lift. It could make Cleveland one of the most attractive cities of America. . . ." But the Halprin Plan, which cost over $300,000, came to nothing.

The final years in this, the most difficult period of the city's history, were marked by political turmoil, a court ruling whose consequences would persist long into the future, and, finally, fiscal crisis. Though Republican Mayor Ralph Perk had built a successful political career by articulating the grievances of his largely ethnic, working-class constituency, the mood of the city was changing. In the 1977 mayoral campaign, Councilman Dennis Kucinich successfully targeted three issues: stopping the proposed sale of the Municipal Electric Light Plant (Muny Light) to the Cleveland Electric Company, ending tax abatement, and the need to concentrate the city's resources on its

George Forbes and Dennis Kucinich became major political figures in Cleveland during the 1970s, with Forbes serving as city council president (1973–1989) and Kucinich as mayor (1977–1979). The Cleveland Press Collection, Cleveland State University.

neighborhoods instead of the downtown. Shortly after taking office, however, the populist mayor, who modeled himself after Mayor Tom L. Johnson, came into conflict with almost every group in the city. His and his young assistants' confrontational style alienated business and civic leaders, the news media, and, ultimately, even those neighborhood groups that had been his chief supporters. Though Kucinich survived a bitter recall election in 1978 by 236 votes, he was swept out of office a year later.

U.S. District Judge Frank J. Battisti, meanwhile, in 1976 ruled that the Cleveland and state boards of education were responsible for the racial segregation of Cleveland schools and must desegregate them. Over a period of thirty-five years, Judge Battisti found, school officials

Cleveland hosted the 49th Annual Convention of the National Association for the Advancement of Colored People in 1959. At that time the local branch of the NAACP was preparing to confront the issues of job discrimination and de facto school segregation. The Cleveland Press Collection, Cleveland State University.

consistently chose to segregate pupils; the state knew about the situation and chose to do nothing about it. The historical problem of segregation in the schools was in part the consequence of segregation in the city's housing patterns. However, since at least the 1930s, school construction plans and decisions with respect to school boundaries and teacher assignments had elicited protests from the black community, many of whom believed that the Board of Education followed an unofficial policy of separating blacks and whites. A major school construction program undertaken by School Superintendent Paul Briggs in the 1960s was perceived as a further attempt to strengthen de facto segregation. The desegregation remedy of crosstown busing helped accelerate a movement from the city of those who could afford a suburban home—blacks as well as whites—while resentment of busing helped defeat levy after levy. By 1980, the Cleveland school system was spending more than $12 million annually on transportation, and enrollment had declined by more than one-third, from 123,000 in 1976 to 81,000.

On 15 December 1978, Cleveland became the first major American city to default since the Depression. The city could not repay $15.5 million in short-term notes that came due, and city officials were unable to agree with local banks on a program to avert default. The default was the product of the dramatic loss of jobs and population—with a consequent shrinkage of the tax base—and a unique political environment in which the mayor's actions were limited by an unwieldy thirty-three-member city council and by citizen demand for low tax rates. The roots of the city's fiscal problems reached back at least as far as 1965, when voters defeated a city income tax referendum, prompting creation of the Cleveland Little Hoover Commission to study city operations. In 1970, when Stokes found that revenues were inadequate to maintain the existing level of city services, he proposed an income tax increase from 1.0 to 1.8 percent, tying it, as an incentive, to a reduction in the school district property tax. Voters turned down the increase but approved the reduction, and at the end of Stokes's second term, the city had a $13-million budget deficit.

Stokes's successor, Ralph Perk, pledged not to seek any tax increases and kept his word. To cover revenue shortfalls, Perk borrowed heavily and tapped bond funds to cover operating deficits. In addition, federal categorical grant programs (including urban renewal) were replaced by community development revenue sharing beginning in 1974, which allowed cities to use the money returned by Washington for locally determined priorities; by 1977, federal aid supported over one-third of the city's budget. Finally, under Perk, the city of Cleveland sold a number of valuable city assets. The sale of its sewage-treatment facilities to a regional authority in 1972 brought in $32 million. Transfer of the Cleveland Transit System to a regional authority in 1975 brought in another $8.9 million. Perk also leased Cleveland Municipal Stadium to private interests and won city council approval of the sale of Muny Light to the Cleveland Electric Illuminating Company, although the latter decision was eventually rescinded.

The sale of assets to cover general debt-service payments and operating costs failed to provide a long-term solution to the city's deteriorating financial condition. Expenditures were increasing rapidly, especially for debt service, while revenues continued to shrink. When Dennis Kucinich was elected mayor in 1977, he faced a critical financial situation: $33 million in short-term debt was to come due by the end of 1978, $15.5 million of which was held by local banks. Kucinich, who had also promised no new taxes, continued to tap bond funds to cover operating expenses. However, he adamantly opposed the sale of city assets and halted the sale of Muny Light. Subsequent suspension of the city's bond rating by Standard & Poor's, and downgrading by Moody's, made it impossible to issue notes to the public to meet continuing obligations. In December 1978, when local banks refused to roll over the city's short-term notes, default became a bleak reality.

It was, to be sure, a period of losses. The city had lost people, business, and industry. It had suffered unprecedented racial strife and the ignominy of default. But decisions to import "name" planners, to lure developers with land writedowns and tax abatement, to advertise the city nationally with such slogans as "The best things in life are here"—all had their roots in Cleveland's most important loss of this period: the loss of confidence.

Cleveland in 1980 was far different from the city that had celebrated the opening of the Union Terminal with such pride a half-century before. Once the nation's sixth-largest city, it was now eighteenth in size; once home to 75 percent of Cuyahoga County residents, it was now home to only 38 percent. By 1930, statistics showed, there already were two Clevelands. And the core of poverty and ring of affluence begun with the streetcar and reinforced by the automobile and the highway were, in 1980, even more pronounced. Neighborhood erosion, epidemic after 1900, was still unabated. And, although a multitude of grassroots conservation efforts were under way, the city remained home to the county's poorest residents, while the economically well-off resided in suburbs that now reached into adjoining counties.

Although the city's historic ethnic groups and their descendants had largely departed for the suburbs, there were still distinct pockets of Italians, Poles, Czechs, Slovenes, Croats, and Hungarians. Foreign-language newspapers, though not so numerous as they had once been, were still published. New Hispanic and Asian immigrants, meanwhile, had come to Cleveland, and their numbers were growing. While residential segregation persisted, blacks no longer were concentrated in crowded ghettos. Indeed, such areas as Hough and Central were now characterized by vast stretches of vacant land, with little prospect that anything would ever be built there. In the 1970s, for the first time, blacks in large numbers had found new homes in the suburbs. East Cleveland was now predominantly black, while Cleveland Heights, Shaker Heights, Garfield Heights, and Euclid all had sizable black populations in 1980. Blacks had made substantial gains in all arenas, but especially in politics. The 21st Congressional District Caucus, organized in the late 1960s, continued to articulate the concerns of black voters. George L. Forbes had begun a long and powerful reign as city council president in 1973, and the city council itself reflected a city now almost half black.

The city struggled, meanwhile, with economic change—with its transition from a blue-collar factory town to one where more than 70 percent were employed in service jobs. Cleveland was growing in importance as a center for education, applied research, and medicine— the Cleveland Clinic Foundation and University Hospitals both ranked among the city's largest employers—and, though Cleveland had dropped in rank, it retained eminence as a corporate-headquarters city. There were signs of interest in redeveloping such areas as the Flats and the Warehouse District, projects that would prove important to Cleveland's economic well-being in the future. But some problems seemed as far from solution as ever. An aging capital plant, few high-income residents, and many high-cost residents were the recipe for ongoing fiscal trouble. Public housing, once the city's pride, was a shambles—often as deteriorated and frightening as the slums it had replaced. Unemployment was high; so was the school dropout rate.

The legacy of highways, urban renewal, poverty, violence, and despair could all be seen in the Cleveland of 1980. Yet, if the city had changed dramatically in the space of half a century, some things remained unchanged. Public Square was still the city's hub, and, despite repeated threats, the Group Plan was still intact. Clevelanders continued to shop at the West Side Market, at the Central Market, and on Coit Road, where farmers from outlying areas still brought their produce. The Flats was still smoky from the remaining mills, the crooked Cuyahoga still crossed by a score of bridges. Blessed as it was with fine museums and theaters, a world-renowned orchestra, and numerous other institutions, Cleveland enjoyed its cultural maturity.

Cleveland's "steady march of progress" (to use the words of William Ganson Rose) had been interrupted—by depression, abandonment, economic decline, racial unrest, and fiscal crisis. But the city retained important advantages, not the least of which were hardworking and generous citizens proud of the city's past and hopeful for its future. The fate of Cleveland, many realized, was not sealed by its past mix of industries and occupations, only influenced by it. The future depended in large part on the intelligence and wisdom with which those who remained would marshal their resources for the betterment of a gritty city determined not only to survive but also to rebuild.

CHAPTER FOURTEEN

Comeback City?

1980–1989

"Cleveland is making a comeback," *Time* magazine announced at the close of 1980. "During the past year, convention business has flourished, school desegregation has proceeded peacefully, and a modest construction boom has begun. . . . Most impressive of all, the city last month dug itself out of default." Foes and friends alike credited George V. Voinovich, the Republican former lieutenant governor who had handily defeated incumbent Dennis Kucinich in the 1979 mayoral election, as the architect of Cleveland's "comeback." While former Mayor Kucinich and his youthful staff had been embroiled in highly publicized conflicts with numerous segments of the community, especially business leaders, Voinovich ushered in an unprecedented ten-year era of cooperation. He patched up relations with the business community, persuading it to donate the services of top executives to analyze city operations. He persuaded local banks to refinance the city's defaulted notes. And, while the fiscal crisis had not passed— "This city is like a house that's been neglected for twelve years," Voinovich said early in his first term—by April 1980 the city had balanced its budget and was prepared to make hard choices, including the layoff of city workers and an appeal for an income tax increase. Political stability improved in November 1981 when Cleveland voters reduced an unwieldy city council from thirty-three to twenty-one members and changed the term of office for both the council and the mayor from two to four years. Cleveland voters reelected Voinovich to the first four-year term by a record 77 percent in 1982, and reelected him again in 1986. When he left office in January 1990, Voinovich had served longer than any other mayor in the city's history.

The road to fiscal recovery was long and painful. Cleveland was $111 million in debt; its credit had been suspended by major Wall Street rating agencies; the state of Ohio had deemed its books "unauditable." The Democratic city council and the Republican mayor cooperated in imposing the stringent policies necessary to escape financial emergency. Community services, from fire stations to swimming pools, were cut and consolidated. Some seven hundred city jobs were eliminated. In February 1981, voters approved an income tax increase from 1.5 percent to 2.0 percent and earmarked half the proceeds for debt repayment and capital improvements. With help from the private sector, the city instituted a new financial management system, while some eighty loaned executives, part of the Mayor's Operations Improvement Task Force, helped streamline city government. In 1983, Cleveland reentered the bond market for the first time since 1978, and on 25 June 1987, the last of the city's debts repaid, the seven-member Financial Planning and Supervision Commission appointed to oversee Cleveland's financial recovery was disbanded. Although default marked what Voinovich called "one of the saddest segments in Cleveland's history," it had forced the city to put its financial house in order, thereby raising the confidence of voters that higher taxes would not be squandered.

Like other cities in the nation's industrial crescent, Cleveland continued to struggle with wrenching economic change. Since the 1960s, the city had watched its heavy industries—steel, automotive products, and machinery—dwindle in the face of foreign competition. In the early 1980s, nationwide recession further eroded the city's traditional economic base. Companies cut back and restructured, leaving thousands of Clevelanders without jobs. Between 1970 and 1985, manufacturing employment in the Cleveland metropolitan area fell by 86,100 jobs (from 296,800 to 210,700 jobs). Over the same period, employment in service industries—especially in the areas of law, health care, and business services—climbed by 76,800 jobs (from 137,500 to 214,300). "The crucible of the 1970s and early 1980s," *Crain's Cleveland Business* reported in 1987, "has forged a new economic mix in Greater Cleveland, one that is much more like that of the nation's." Whereas manufacturing accounted for 47 percent of all jobs in Greater Cleveland (24 percent nationally) in 1970, by 1987 manufacturing provided just 27 percent of Greater Cleveland's jobs (compared to 20 percent nationally). This economic restructuring was not without cost. "There is . . . a deeply troubling side to the onset of the service economy," *Crain's* acknowledged. "Cleveland's traditional blue-collar work force isn't participating in it. And those service jobs that the former factory workers can fill generally pay less than their old jobs."

With the loss of industry, Cleveland and Cuyahoga County were home to large numbers of people the emerging economy had passed by, and who were increasingly dependent on government. "For the first time," said Timothy Hagan, president of the Cuyahoga County Board of Commissioners, "we have in our midst a permanent underclass." The economic dislocation was not proportionate: in 1987, unemployment within the city of Cleveland was 11.4 percent, more than double the suburban rate of 5.4 percent. Young people, especially minorities, were hardest hit.

Cleveland in the 1980s was typical (except in degree) of many declining cities in the Northeast and Midwest regions of the nation. Decreasing population was a fact of life. The city's population had dropped a precipitous 23 percent between 1970 and 1980. In the 1980s, the rate of loss slowed to about 1 percent annually but showed no sign of abating. In 1989, urban analyst Thomas Bier reported that the city was losing approximately 3,500 households each year; most of those leaving the city were middle-income families with children relocating to the suburbs. Cuyahoga County's population, too, was declining, though at a slower rate. The continuing shrinkage was underscored by the 1982 closing of Halle's, the Euclid Avenue department store that had catered to the city's carriage trade since 1891, and by the demise, on 17 June 1982, of the *Cleveland Press*. The longtime

flagship of the Scripps-Howard chain had been "rescued" by millionaire merchant Joseph E. Cole in 1980 but continued to lose money.
Its closing, part of a trend that saw the demise of afternoon dailies
nationwide, left Cleveland a one-newspaper town. A shrinking tax
base, meanwhile, led the city to lease its lakefront parks (Edgewater,
Gordon, and Wildwood) to the state of Ohio, which refurbished them
to form the new Cleveland Lakefront State Park. The city also transferred Garfield Park, the Cleveland Aquarium, and the Cleveland Zoo
to Cleveland Metroparks, a metropolitan agency with a broader tax
base.

Despite a declining population, Cleveland witnessed a remarkable
building boom downtown during these years. Standard Oil Company
(acquired by BP America and renamed in 1987), Ohio Bell, and Eaton
Corporation all built new office towers. The national real-estate community discovered Cleveland, too. Developers who had previously confined their investments to suburban locations now launched important
projects downtown. Brothers Richard and David Jacobs, principals in
the Westlake-based Jacobs, Visconsi & Jacobs Company, astonished
Cleveland by rescuing the troubled Cleveland Indians franchise,
building the glass-roofed Galleria at Erieview, with two levels of styl-
ish shops, and planning the construction of two megabuildings—the
fifty-five-story Society Center (under construction in 1989) and the
sixty-story Ameritrust Center—each housing a hotel and offices. Forest City Enterprises embarked on a massive reconstruction of Cleveland's historic Union Terminal; Tower City Center, slated to open in
1990, would encompass new retail stores and offices, a rebuilt rapid-
transit station, and a luxury hotel. Civic boosters looked to the new
hotels, together with the $28-million renovation of the Cleveland Con-
vention Center, to aid Cleveland's bid once again to become an important convention city.

There were other signals of confidence in the area's economic future: the Cleveland Clinic expansion, the new TRW headquarters in
Lyndhurst, and the 1988 announcement by Figgie International that
it would build a new corporate headquarters on city-owned land in
Warrensville Township as part of a $500-million mixed-use develop-
ment. While facing increasing competition from suburban develop-

ments, especially the office nodes that had sprung up along Chagrin Boulevard and Rockside Road, downtown Cleveland remained the office hub of the region, and its economic well-being during these years served as a catalyst for important redevelopment projects.

Spurred by new tax incentives for the rehabilitation of historic buildings, there was renewed interest in the city's historic Warehouse District. There, nineteenth-century commercial buildings were turned into offices, loft apartments, and new shops and restaurants. At Playhouse Square, the ambitious theater restoration project launched in 1975 was now a showcase for civic pride, as well as a stimulus to local economic development. The restored Ohio, State, and Palace theaters (the future of the Allen remained uncertain) were home to theater, ballet, dance, and an array of popular entertainment. According to a 1985 study by the Federal Reserve Bank, Playhouse Square Center brought $15 million to the Cleveland economy each year.

Redevelopment of the waterfront became another important piece of the city's economic strategy during the decade. Cleveland looked to Lake Erie and the Cuyahoga River to attract people and business back to the city. In the Flats, entrepreneurs transformed old warehouses and factories into trendy restaurants, shops, and nightclubs. On summer weekends, the Cuyahoga River was thick with pleasure boats. On the lakefront, meanwhile, state, city, and private funds combined to complete the first phase of the North Coast Harbor—a protected basin with pleasure-boat moorings and a waterside promenade at the foot of East 9th Street—in 1988. Planners hoped the new amenities, including a proposed aquarium and Great Lakes museum, would lure new commercial and residential development.

Most of the new investment downtown was publicly subsidized, leveraged by some $132 million in Urban Development Action Grants the city won from the U.S. Department of Housing and Urban Development during these years. Some projects—Society Center, Ameritrust Center, and the hotel at Tower City—enjoyed the additional award of twenty-year property tax abatement, which opponents argued would deprive city schools of substantial future income. Did tax abatement unnecessarily reward wealthy developers who would have built their projects anyway? The question was the subject of continuing debate. Less controversial was the city's program of granting seven-year tax abatement for new and substantially renovated housing, which stimulated the construction of new middle-income housing—Lexington Village in the Hough neighborhood, for example, and The Triangle at University Circle—that otherwise might not have been built.

Glittering new development downtown brought with it the perceptible return of civic pride. "Trolley" tours and a succession of fairs and festivals brought Greater Clevelanders downtown and to the Flats. Even Cleveland's professional sports teams rebounded, with the Browns and the Cavaliers winning playoff berths, and the Indians drawing 1.5 million during the 1986 season, the highest attendance since 1959. The psychological renewal was largely confined to downtown, however, as the city's neighborhoods continued to erode, losing people, jobs, and housing. As in big cities nationwide, drugs (and drug-related crime) became Cleveland's single most serious problem. A glut of housing in inner-ring suburbs, meanwhile, drew many Cleveland families, including many blacks, out of the city. Some city neighborhoods lost their longtime ethnic identity. But there was also a modest infusion of new immigrants. The city's Chinese community, clustered at East 40th Street and Payne Avenue, was growing, as were the numbers of Vietnamese and Cambodians, most of whom settled on the near West Side. A small influx of Poles, meanwhile, settled in the Slavic Village neighborhood.

Bottom-up, grass-roots renewal efforts continued during these years, though neighborhood advocacy groups, organized in the 1960s and 1970s around such issues as unfair treatment by banks and insurance companies and inadequate city services, declined in the 1980s from lack of funding. The work of rebuilding neighborhoods shifted to local development corporations. Focusing on brick-and-mortar projects, groups like the Slavic Village Association, the Detroit-Shoreway Community Development Organization, and the Clark-Metro Development Corporation became instruments for neighborhood commercial, industrial, and residential redevelopment.

At decade's end, an improved national economy, local economic development initiatives, and growth in the service sector had helped stabilize area employment. But poverty continued to tighten its grip on the city even as it widened its reach to inner-ring suburbs like Lakewood, East Cleveland, and Cleveland Heights. In 1989, the Council for Economic Opportunities in Greater Cleveland reported that poverty in Cuyahoga County had increased by 42.5 percent since 1980; that almost one-fifth of all county residents were poor; and that three-quarters of the county's poor (or about 215,700 people) lived in the city of Cleveland. Race relations, meanwhile, remained uneasy, and incidents of racial violence increased.

While Mayor George Voinovich generally was credited with bringing continuity and competence to city government, he was also criticized for yielding too much authority to the strong-willed city council president, George L. Forbes. Agencies outside the mayor's purview but nonetheless critical to the city's welfare—the Regional Transit Authority, the Cuyahoga Metropolitan Housing Authority, and the Cleveland Public Schools—worsened during these years. RTA annual ridership plummeted from nearly 123 million in 1978 to 75 million in 1988—a 39 percent decline. The agency was plagued by mismanagement, low morale, and political patronage. Meanwhile, more than 17,000 Clevelanders were living in what one federal housing official described as "the second-worst public housing" in the nation. Public housing operated by the Cuyahoga Metropolitan Housing Authority was beset by crime, inadequate maintenance, and mismanagement. Between 1980 and 1989, the vacancy rate climbed from 10 percent to 25 percent; some housing projects were controlled by drug dealers. Although these conditions periodically drew the attention of politicians and the media, there was no meaningful improvement.

Many continued to view the Cleveland public schools as among the community's foremost problems. In 1980, Federal Judge Frank Battisti attacked the school board for "maladministration, a form of resistance quite different from standing in the schoolhouse door, but equally effective." He placed the school district in what amounted to receivership, dividing its management between the school board and a court-appointed administrator of desegregation. In 1985, Dr. Frederick ("Doc") Holliday, who had come to Cleveland in 1982 as the school district's first black superintendent, fatally shot himself in the chest in a stairwell of a city school. "The fighting among school board members and what petty politics is doing to the system has sickened me," Holliday wrote in his suicide note. Political infighting continued, however, while declining enrollment and a 70 percent black majority in the classrooms (it was 60 percent a decade earlier) suggested that desegregation had not fulfilled its promises. In 1987, Cleveland business leaders initiated a "dollars for scholars" program to help improve a school dropout rate that now approached 50 percent. "We are not an asset," Cleveland School Board President Joseph G. Tegreene acknowledged in 1986. "And until the Cleveland schools improve, there cannot be an appreciable revitalization of the city."

Partly in reaction to the renewed interest of developers, the Cleveland City Planning Commission in 1989 adopted a new master plan, "Cleveland Civic Vision 2000," to guide land use and development into the twenty-first century; the name of the plan derived from a speech by visiting developer James Rouse, who urged his City Club audience to adopt a "civic vision" for Cleveland. In 1989, many other ambitious plans were on the drawing board. The hard-won Rock-and-Roll Hall of Fame and Museum, projected for completion in 1992 (and for which the city agreed to raise $40 million of its $48 million price tag), was expected to attract 600,000 visitors a year. Despite a shrinking population, transit planners eyed a downtown subway and a new rail link between downtown Cleveland and University Circle, estimated to cost $567 million. And, although Cuyahoga County voters in 1984 rejected, by a 2-to-1 margin, a proposed property-tax levy to finance construction of a domed stadium, proponents of the plan proceeded, forming the Greater Cleveland Domed Stadium Corporation and borrowing $22 million from banks and the state of Ohio to purchase a site. By 1989, 28 acres in the Central Market area had been cleared of buildings (and businesses) and made into parking lots, although there still was no firm plan in hand for financing the project. A stadium, a subway, a rock-and-roll hall of fame—all, it seemed, were a lot simpler to conceive and accomplish than decent, affordable housing or the revival of a city neighborhood.

In 1989, civic leaders could say, cautiously, that Cleveland's long downward spiral had been reversed. Headlines around the country seemed to confirm it: "Cleveland Comes Back!" (*Reader's Digest*), "City Rebounds from Ugly Image" (*Cincinnati Enquirer*), "Cleveland: Maligned, Scoffed At, This Midwest City Has Bounced Back" (*Christian Science Monitor*). The stories told of a city turning itself around, a city of robust new development, a city with a future much brighter than could have been predicted a decade ago. But behind the headlines was another city. The dichotomy was aptly described by a reporter for the *Washington Post*, who wrote in 1986: "The New Cleveland is corporate headquarters, service and professional jobs, downtown construction, recreational and cultural amenities. The Old Cleveland is neighborhoods struggling against decay, double-digit unemployment, racial tension, factory closings, poverty and long-suffering schools."

Cleveland in the 1980s had simultaneously expanded and contracted, and the by-products of a painful transition would be visible for a long time to come. For even as developers reshaped the city's skyline, Clevelanders lacking the skills appropriate to the new technology-based service economy faced a dismal future. The homeless and the hungry were conspicuous. Indeed, bridging the gap between rich and poor would remain a central issue. Who—the question begged to be asked—would the new "civic vision" include? And who would be left out?

CPM

INDEX

Academy of Music, 59, 86
Alhambra Theater, 115
Aliened American, 56
Allen, John W., 46
Allen Theater, 114, 186
Alta House, 92, 93
Amalgamated Association of Street Car
    Men, 89
Ambler Heights, 103
American Colonization Society, 43
American House, 99
American Steel & Wire Division of
    United States Steel Corporation, 71. *See
    also* Cleveland Rolling Mill
Ameritrust Center, 185, 186
Angle, The, 86
Appalachians, 147
Arcade, The, 96
Asian Immigrants, 180
Atlantic & Great Western Railroad, 70

BP America, Inc., 185
Badger, Joseph, 17
Baehr, Herman C., 108–09
Bailey's Department Store, 101, 115, 142,
    167
Baker, Newton D., 108–09, 112
Baker Motor Vehicle Company, 116
Battisti, Frank J., 176, 188
Battle of Fallen Timbers, 8
Bellamy, George A., 92
Bethel Associated Charities, 91
Bethel Union, 72, 91
Big Italy, 103
Birdtown, 86
Blacks, 39–40, 43, 55–56, 72, 86,
    105–06, 110, 113, 121, 133, 135–36,
    147, 180
Board of Trade, 59, 94. *See also* Cleveland
    Chamber of Commerce; Greater Cleve-
    land Growth Association
Bohemians. *See* Czechs
Bohn, Ernest J., 139
Bond Court Building, 164
Bowditch, Ernest, 94
Bradley, Alva, 80
Bratenahl, 103
Briggs, Paul, 177
Brooklyn, 147, 158
Brooklyn Township, 47, 78
Brooks, Charles S., 79
Brotherhood of Locomotive Engineers,
    115

Brotherhood of Locomotive Firemen and
    Enginemen, 116
Brotherhood of Railroad Trainmen, 116
Brown, Alexander E., 80
Brown, John Harkness, 96
Brush, Charles Francis, 154
Builders' Exchange Building, 129
Burke, Thomas A., 152
Burnham, Daniel, 108
Burton, Harold H., 142
Butterfield, Zethan, 9

Calhoun, Patrick, 96
Cambodians, 187
Camp Cleveland, 74–75
Canadians, 133
Carter, Lorenzo, 14, 17
Carver Park, 154
Case, Leonard, 24
Case, Leonard Jr., 96
Case School, 96
Case Western Reserve University, School
    of Applied Social Sciences, 151
Cedar-Central Apartments, 140
Celebrezze, Anthony J., 157
Central Area, 162, 180
Central Avenue Viaduct, 94
Central Friendly Inn, 92
Central High School, 96
Central Market, 181, 189
Central-Woodland Neighborhood, 92, 103
Chandler-Cleveland Motors Corp., 116
Charity Organization Society, 91
Chesnutt, Charles W., 135
Chester Commons, 174
Chinese, 187
Chisholm, Henry, 71
Chisholm, William, 88–89
Chisholm, Jones & Company, 71
Circle Theater, 115
Citizen, The, 91
Citizens League, 93, 120
City Infirmary, 60
City manager, 120, 142
Civil War, 69, 72, 74, 76
Civil Works Administration, 136, 138
Clark-Fulton Neighborhood, 102
Clark-Metro Development Corporation,
    187
Cleaveland, Moses, 8–9, 23
Cleveland Americanization Committee,
    104
Cleveland & Pittsburgh Railroad, 71–72

Cleveland Aquarium, 185
Cleveland Architectural Club, 108
Cleveland Board of Education, 60, 177
Cleveland Board of Education Building,
    130
Cleveland Browns, 187
Cleveland Cavaliers, 187
Cleveland Centennial Commission, 99
Cleveland Chamber of Commerce, 102,
    108, 109, 121, 147, 157; Convention
    Board, 130
Cleveland Chess Club, 59
Cleveland City Council, 73
Cleveland City Hospital Society, 72
Cleveland City Planning Commission,
    162, 163, 171, 174, 189
Cleveland City Railway Company, 94
"Cleveland Civic Vision 2000," 189
Cleveland Clinic Foundation, 180, 185
Cleveland Community Fund, 110
Cleveland Community Relations Board,
    152, 158
Cleveland Convention and Visitors Bu-
    reau, 154
Cleveland Convention Center, 166, 185
Cleveland Cricket Club, 59
Cleveland Cultural Gardens, 145
Cleveland Development Foundation, 165
Cleveland Electric Illuminating Com-
    pany, 149, 179
Cleveland Electric Light Company, 175
Cleveland Electric Railway Company, 94,
    108
Cleveland Forum, 22
Cleveland Foundation, 110, 175
Cleveland Grays, 44, 74
Cleveland Guards, 44
Cleveland Heights, 102, 118, 130, 131,
    134, 147, 157, 159, 180, 188
Cleveland Hopkins International Airport,
    113–14, 130, 148
Cleveland Indians, 115, 143, 154, 185,
    187
Cleveland Industrial Exposition of 1909,
    101
Cleveland Institute of Art, 96
Cleveland Institute of Music, 118
Cleveland Iron Mining Company, 79
Cleveland Lakefront State Park, 185
Cleveland Library Association, 59
Cleveland Medical College, 45, 96
Cleveland Memorial Shoreway, 138
Cleveland Mendelssohn Society, 43
Cleveland Metroparks, 138, 185
Cleveland Metropolitan Housing Author-
    ity, 139

Cleveland Metropolitan Park District, 114
Cleveland Municipal Stadium, 130, 143,
    178
Cleveland Museum of Art, 117
Cleveland Museum of Natural History,
    118
Cleveland Music School Settlement, 118
Cleveland Orchestra, 117, 145
Cleveland Play House, 118
Cleveland Police Department, 73
Cleveland Public Library, 105, 130
Cleveland Public Schools, 188–89
Cleveland Railway Company, 108, 152
Cleveland Reading Room, 43
Cleveland Real Estate Board, 121
Cleveland Rolling Mill, 71–72, 83, 88
Cleveland School of Art, 96
Cleveland School of Music, 96
Cleveland Spiders, 98
Cleveland Suffrage League, 110
Cleveland Temperance Alliance, 58
Cleveland Township, 21–22
Cleveland Transit System, 152, 157, 174,
    178
Cleveland Trust Company, 110
Cleveland Union Stockyards, 150
Cleveland Union Terminal, 116, 129
Cleveland Welfare Federation, 110
Cleveland, Columbus & Cincinnati Rail-
    road (CC&C), 50–51, 52
Cleveland: NOW!, 169
Clifton Park, 96, 103
Clinton Square, 36
Cole, Joseph E., 185
Coliseum, 173
Collinwood, 83, 100, 103
Colored Association of Cleveland, 55
Colored Young Men's Union Society, 55
Columbus Street Bridge, 47–48
Commercial Bank of Lake Erie, 26
Commerical Coffee House, 23
Committee on Benevolent Associations,
    109
Community Relations Board, 158
Connecticut Land Company, 7–8, 10, 15
Consumers League of Ohio, 110
Corrigan, McKinney Steel Corporation,
    142
Council for Economic Opportunities in
    Greater Cleveland, 188
Crittenden House, 41
Croatians, 83, 180
Cuyahoga Building, 97
Cuyahoga Community College, 162
Cuyahoga County, 16, 26, 33, 69, 70, 75,
    82, 118, 136, 157, 159

Cuyahoga County Board of Commissioners, 184
Cuyahoga County Relief Administration, 137
Cuyahoga Metropolitan Housing Authority, 188
Cuyahoga River, 7, 8, 19, 31, 73, 78, 81, 85, 95, 154, 186
Cuyahoga Steam Furnace Company, 38
Czechs, 72, 82–83, 88, 101, 131, 180

Davis, Harry L., 120, 142
Default, 178
Democratic Party, 46
Depression of the 1930s, 142–43, 146, 147
Detroit-Shoreway Community Development Organization, 187
Doan, Nathaniel, 14
Doan's Corners, 78, 102
"Downtown Cleveland 1975," 162
Dunham Tavern, Inc., 145
Dutch Hill, 86

Early Settlers' Association, 99
East Cleveland, 78, 130, 131, 134, 157, 180, 188
East Cleveland Railway Company, 74
Eastgate Shopping Center, 159
Eaton Corporation, 185
Eberhard Manufacturing Company, 81
Edgewater Park, 185
Elysium Ice Palace, 115
English Immigrants, 82, 133
Enterprise, 27
Erieview, 156, 161–64, 166
Erieview Tower, 164
Ernst & Ernst, 165
Euclid, 158, 180
Euclid Avenue, 56, 70, 72, 79, 96, 155
Euclid Avenue Opera House, 97–98, 115
Euclid Beach Park, 98, 102
Euclid Street Presbyterian Church, City Mission, 59
Evans, Fred (Ahmed), 169
Everett, Henry A., 89
Express Highway Subcommittee, 152

F.B. Stearns Company, 116
Fairmount Reservoir, 94
Fairview Park, 158
Father Mathew Total Abstinence Society, 55
Federal Building, 164
Federal Emergency Relief Administration, 137
Federal Knitting Mills, 104

Federal Plan, 93, 109
Federal Reserve Bank, 130, 186
Federation for Charity and Philanthropy, 109
Federation of Organized Trades and Labor Unions, 89
Ferry Cap & Screw, 104
Figgie International, Inc., 185
Financial Planning and Supervision Commission, 183
First Ohio Volunteer Infantry, 74
First Presbyterian Church, 44, 92
Fisher Aircraft Assembly Plant No. 2, 148
Fisher Body Company, 116, 142
Five Points, 102
Flats, The, 41, 70, 78, 173, 180, 181, 186, 187
Forbes, George L., 180, 188
Forest City Enterprises, 185
Forest City House, 99
Franklin Circle, 54
Freemasons, 17
Free-Soil Party, 58
Friendly Inn Social Settlement, 92

Galbreath, John W., 164
Galleria, 185
Gannett, Alice, 92, 110
Garden Center of Greater Cleveland, 145
Garden Valley Housing Association, 162
Garden Valley Neighborhood, 161
Garfield, Harry, A., 93
Garfield Building, 97
Garfield Heights, 118, 180
Garfield Park, 185
Geauga County, 16
General Plan of 1949, 162
George, Clayborne, 123
German Guards, 54
Germans, 39, 44, 46, 53–55, 56, 63, 82, 120, 131, 135
Giddings, Joshua B., 58
Gladstone, 161–62
Glenville, 96, 100, 147–48, 162, 169
Glenville Community Council, 148
Glenville Shoot-out, 169
Goff, Frederick H., 110
Golden Gate Shopping Center, 159
Goodrich House, 92, 110
Goodrich-Gannett Neighborhood Center, 92
Gordon Park, 185
Granger, Gideon, 17
Grasselli Chemical Company, 81
Great Lakes Exposition, 143–44

Greater Cleveland Council of Smaller Business of America, Inc., 148
Greater Cleveland Domed Stadium Corp., 189
Greater Cleveland Growth Association, 174, 175
Greater Cleveland Regional Transit Authority, 174, 188
Greeks, 83
Gregg, E. J., 123
Group Plan, 94, 100, 108, 109, 113, 130, 143–44, 180
Gun, Elijah, 19

Halle Brothers Company, 101, 184
Halprin Plan, 175
Haltnorth's Gardens, 98
Hanna Building, 130
Hanna Theater, 114–15
Harris, Jessie, 21
Harris-Intertype Corporation, 172
Hathaway Brown, 96
Hawley, Ezekiel, 14
Hay, John, 88
Hayes, Max S., 91
Haymarket District, 84, 86, 92, 116
Heckewelder, John, 7
Herrick, Rensselaer R., 95
Hibernerian Guards, 55
Higbee Company, 123, 129, 173
Hiram House, 92
Hispanic Immigrants, 180
Hitchcock, Peter, 24
Hollenden House, 99
Holliday, Frederick, 188
Hopkins, William R., 120, 130, 143
Hotel Cleveland, 116, 129
Hough, 98, 147, 162, 166–67, 180, 187
Hough Area Council, 166
Hough Riots, 165, 168
Howard, John T., 162
Howe, Federick C., 78
Hulett, George H., 80
Hungarians, 82–83, 103, 131, 147, 180
Hunter, Jane Edna, 110–11
Huntington, Samuel, 17
Huran Road Mall, 174

Independent Order of Good Templars, 58
Indians (Native), 8
Industrial Rayon Corporation, 142
Industrial School, 60
International Order of Odd Fellows, 44, 59
Irish, 39, 46, 53–55, 56, 82, 133, 135, 147

Irish Naturalization Society of Cleveland, 55
Italians, 83, 92, 101, 103, 106, 131, 135, 180
Ivanhoe Boat Club, 59

Jacobs, Visconsi & Jacobs Company, 185
Jews, 82, 103, 106, 135
John Carroll University, 96
Johnson, Tom L., 100, 106–08, 112, 176
Joseph & Feiss Company, 104
Junior League of Cleveland, Inc., 174

Karamu House, 118
Keith's 105th Street Theater, 115
Kelley, Alfred, 25, 31
Kelly, Daniel, 24
Kentucky Street Reservoir, 61, 72–73
King Iron Bridge & Manufacturing Company, 82
Kingsbury, James, 14
Kingsbury Run, 81, 83
Kinsman Reservoir, 94
Know-Nothing Party, 63
Kohler, Fred, 130
Kouba Neighborhood, 86
Krumholz, Norman, 174
Kucinich, Dennis, 175–76, 179, 182
Kundtz, Theodor, 84

Ladies' Aid Society, 76
Lake Erie, 7, 25, 32, 78, 186
Lake Shore & Michigan Southern Railroad, 83, 87
Lake Shore Rolling Mill, 72
Lake Theater, 114
Lakeview Terrace, 141
Lakewood, 96, 118, 130, 131, 134, 157, 188
Laurel School, 96
Lausche, Frank J., 150, 154
Law, Jonathan, 7, 16, 19
League Park, 98, 115, 143
Ledbetter, Eleanor E., 104
Leonard C. Hanna Fund, 166
Lexington Village, 187
Library Association, 43
Lincoln, Abraham, 63, 74, 76
Lindseth, Elmer L., 156
Lister, James M., 161
Little Hoover Commission, 168, 178
Little Italy, 103
Little Steel Strike of 1937, 142
Locher, Ralph S., 167
Longwood, 160

Luna Park, 106, 141
Lyndhurst, 147, 158

McKisson, Robert E., 93
Mahoning Canal, 49
Main Avenue Bridge, 138
Mall, 108, 143–44, 145, 166, 174. *See also* Group Plan
Maple Heights, 147, 158
Martha Washington and Dorcas Society, 44
Maschke, Maurice, 109
Masons, 43, 59
Mather, Flora Stone, 92
Mather, Samuel, 79, 93
Mather, Samuel Livingston, 79
May, T. P., 46
May Company, 101
May Day, 1894, 91
May Day, 1919, 120
Mayfield Heights, 147, 158
Mayo, Leonard, 151
Mayor's Operations Improvement Task Force, 183
Mechanics' Lyceum, 42
Medical Arts Building, 129
Melodeon Hall, 74
Merwin's Hotel, 23
Metropolitan Police Act, 73
Midland Building, 129
Miles Heights, 118, 147
Miller, Ray T., 136, 142
Millionaires' Row, 155. *See also* Euclid Avenue
Morgan, Daniel E., 120
Mount Pleasant, 147, 162
Mozart Society, 43
Municipal Electric Light Plant (Muny Light), 175, 179
Murray Hill, 93, 103

NASA Lewis Research Center, 149
National Advisory Committee for Aeronautics (NACA), 149
National Association for the Advancement of Colored People, 123
National City Bank Building, 175
National Screw & Manufacturing Company, 171
Ness, Eliot, 142
New England Building, 97
New York Central Railroad, 133
New York, Chicago & St. Louis Railroad, 133
Newburgh, 16, 72, 83
Newburgh Township, 78

Nickel Plate Railroad, 116, 125. *See also* New York, Chicago & St. Louis Railroad
North American Saengerfest, 54
North Coast Harbor, 186
Norton, David Z., 93

Oberlin-Wellington Rescue, 58
Ohio & Erie Canal, 31–32, 34, 49
Ohio Bell Telephone Company, 130, 185
Ohio City, 38–39, 42, 47–48, 49, 53, 62–63, 72, 163
Ohio Light Artillery, 99
Ohio Theater, 114, 186
Old Stone Church. *See* First Presbyterian Church
Olney, Charles E., 108
Outhwaite Homes, 141, 154

Palace Theater, 114, 186
Palda, Leopold J., 88
Panic of 1818, 26
Panic of 1837, 36
Panic of 1873, 87
Panic of 1893, 91
Parma, 118, 158
Parmatown Shopping Center, 159
Payne, Henry B., 72
Pease, Seth, 9
Peerless Motor Car Company, 116
Perk, Ralph J., 175, 178
Perry, Horace, 24
Perry, Oliver Hazard, statue of, 70
Phillis Wheatley Association, 111
Pickands, Mather & Company, 79
Playhouse Settlement. *See* Karamu House
Playhouse Square, 114, 130, 163, 167, 174, 186
Polemic Association, 43
Poles, 82, 88, 101, 103, 131, 180, 187
Postwar Planning Council, 150, 154–55
Protestant Orphan Asylum, 59
Public Auditorium, 113, 130
Public Square, 27, 41, 44, 61, 69–70, 72, 76, 78, 92, 99, 113, 116, 125, 129, 145, 154, 162, 175, 181
Public Utilities Building, 164
Public Works Administration, 139
Public Works of Art Project, 139
Puerto Ricans, 147
Puritas Springs Park, 98

Ragged School, 59, 60
Real Property Inventory of Greater Cleveland, 135, 171
Republic Steel Corporation, 142
Ritchie, Ryerson, 109

"Roaring Third," 123
Rock-and-Roll Hall of Fame and Museum, 189
Rockefeller, John D., 75, 80–81, 93
Rockefeller Building, 101, 145
Rockefeller Park, 145
Rockport, 102
Rocky River, 102
Rose, William Grey, 87
Rouse, James, 189
Russians, 82, 131, 135
Ruthenburg, Charles F., 120

St. Clair Neighborhood, 102
St. Ignatius College, 96
St. Mary's on the Flats, 44
St. Vincent Center, 160, 162
St. Vincent Charity Hospital, 72
Scots, 39, 72, 133
Serbians, 83
Settlers' Landing, 173
Severance, John L., 117
Severance Center, 159
Severance Hall, 117, 145
Shaker Heights, 116, 118, 120, 130, 131, 134, 180
Shaker Square, 142, 159
Shaker Village, 113
Shakespeare Gallery, 22
Shepardson, Ray K., 174
Sheriff Street Market, 97
Sherwin, Belle, 110
Sherwin, John, 93
Skarda, Frank, 88
Slavic Village, 187
Sloane, John, 24
Slovaks, 83
Slovenes, 83, 180
Society Center, 185, 186
Society for Savings Building, 96
Society for the Relief of the Poor, 59
Soldiers' Aid Society of Northern Ohio, 75
Sons of Malta, 59
Sons of Temperance, 58
South Brooklyn, 100, 102
South Euclid, 147, 158
Southgate Shopping Center, 159
Spafford, Amos, 9
Standard Oil Company, 79, 81, 83, 85, 87, 185
State Theater, 114, 174, 186
Sterling & Welch Company, 101
Sterling-Lindner Department Store, 167
Stillman Theater, 114
Stinchcomb, William A., 114
Stokes, Carl B., 169, 178

Stone, Amasa, 56, 72, 88, 96
Stone, Andros, 72
Stouffer's Inn on the Square, 175
Superior Avenue Viaduct, 94

TRW, Inc., 185
Taft, Seth, 169
Tayler, Robert W., 108
Tayler Grant, The, 108
Tegreene, Joseph G., 189
Terminal Tower, 113, 124, 129, 154
Thompson Aircraft Products Company, 148
Tower City Center, 185, 186
Treasury Relief Art Project, 141
Tremont, 72, 84
Triangle (University Circle), 187
Trinity Cathedral, 99
Trinity Church, 36
Tullis, Richard B., 172
21st Congressional District Caucus, 180

Union Depot, 70
Union Terminal, 125, 185
United States General Hospital, 75
University Circle, 96, 163, 187, 189
University Circle, Inc., 163
University Heights, 74
University Hospitals, 72, 180
University School, 96
University Theater, 115
University-Euclid Urban-Renewal Project, 167

Valley View Homes, 141
Van-Aken Warrensville Shopping Center, 159
Van Dorn Iron Works Company, 82
Van Sweringen, Mantis J. and Oris P., 116, 124, 129, 130, 152, 159
Van Sweringen Company, 116
Veeck, Bill, 154
Vietnamese, 187
Vlchek Tool Company, 85
Voinovich, George V., 182–83, 188

Wade, Jeptha H., 72
Wade Park, 117, 163
Wags of Cleveland, 22
Walk-in-the-Water, 27
Walworth, Ashbel, 24
Walworth Run Foundry Company, 82
War of 1812, 22, 26
War Service Center, 154
Warehouse District, 180, 186
Warrensville Township, 102, 185
Warszawa, 86, 103

Washingtonians, 58
Waterman, Eleazar, 24
Weizer, John, 103
Welsh Immigrants, 72, 133
West Cleveland, 78
West Park, 118
West Side Market, 108, 181
Western Reserve, 7, 10, 16, 53, 78
Western Reserve Building, 96–97
Western Reserve College, 96
Western Reserve University. *See* Case
  Western University
Westgate Shopping Center, 159
Weston, S. Burns, 150
Whig Party, 45, 46, 58
Whig-Free-Soil-Independent Democratic
  Party, 58
White Motor Company, 116
White Sewing Machine Company, 84
Wildwood Park, 185
Willey, John, 44
Willeyville, 36

William Taylor Department Store, 167
Wing, Marie Remington, 110
Winton, Alexander, 154
Winton Motor Car Company, 116
Witt, Stillman, 72
Woman's Christian Temperance League,
  91
Women's Department of the Centennial
  Commission, 99
Wood, Reuben, 23
Woodhill Homes, 141
Woodland Avenue Street Railroad, 74
Woodland-Broadway Neighborhood, 124
Woodland-Central Neighborhood, 123
Works Progress Administration, 137–38
World War II, 142, 147
Worley, David, 46

Young, Cy, 98
Young Men's Christian Association, 123
Young Women's Christian Association,
  72, 111–12, 123